COFFEE
ROASTER'S
HANDBOOK

COFFEE ROASTER'S HANDBOOK

A HOW-TO GUIDE FOR HOME AND PROFESSIONAL ROASTERS

LEN BRAULT

callisto
publishing
an imprint of Sourcebooks

To my patient and
gentle wife, Pearl,
for her support
and sage advice.

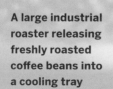
A large industrial roaster releasing freshly roasted coffee beans into a cooling tray

Contents

Introduction

One of my earliest memories is smelling the wonderful coffee brewing in a glass percolator on my mother's stovetop. Of course, this beverage was for adults and I never actually tasted it. At the age of 16, my first job was at an Anton's Cleaners located next to a Friendly's restaurant—it occurred to me here that I was now a young adult and maybe I should actually try *drinking* coffee. I loaded that cup of coffee from Friendly's with half-and-half and sugar, I took a sip, and a coffee addict was born.

Through the years, I enjoyed frequenting creative coffee shops, such as the Coffee Connection chain in Massachusetts, and bemoaned its loss when it was purchased by a large conglomerate and turned into coffee shops that sold burnt, unidimensional coffee. Left to my own devices, I haunted import shops and tried blending Café Caribe, Café Bustelo, Melitta, and Lavazza coffees and was generally able to keep my employees and myself happy with the office coffee. However, it seemed as time wore on, it became harder and harder to find great-quality coffee.

In 2005, I learned about a popular brand of Vietnamese coffee and managed to become the exclusive online distributor for the United

States and Canada. I had married a wonderful Filipina who introduced me to Liberica (Barako coffee) from her native Batangas, and I went on to specialize in importing Southeast Asian coffees from the Philippines, Vietnam, Indonesia, Myanmar, and more. I realized that coffees from these regions had not been subjected to much meddling from American conglomerate coffee companies to hybridize and standardize only one variety. Farmers were growing older, more diverse species and varieties. This is important, because monoculture in the current times of climate change will only lead to more coffee blights and possible extinctions of entire genetic strains.

I am the type of person who cannot stand not knowing something about a thing I love, so I began to research, study, and travel to learn everything I could about coffee history, cultivation, and brewing. I began to realize that coffee—the second-most traded commodity in the world—had an enormous capacity to change the economic well-being of more than a billion people across the globe. All it took was responsible buying practices from consumers in the United States, the country that consumes the most cups of coffee in the world each year. It has become my personal mission to pass on my knowledge in the hope of bringing coffee joy into consumers' lives and to assist in raising the standard of living for the producers of this wonderful beverage.

In this book I have worked hard to remember all the questions I've encountered and all the decisions I made when first learning how to roast. I've addressed the concerns of everyone who wants to roast—whether using an air popper or a large commercial roaster—and provided a body of knowledge that is not generally available anywhere else. I hope you enjoy reading this roasting guide as much as I enjoyed writing it!

A rainbow of coffee cherries, green coffee beans, and roasted coffee beans

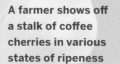

A farmer shows off a stalk of coffee cherries in various states of ripeness

PART I: GETTING TO KNOW COFFEE

A vintage illustration depicting a scene from a coffee plantation in Brazil

CHAPTER 1
A BRIEF HISTORY OF COFFEE

Ancient Coffee History—Spiritual Healers, Romans, and Muhammad

Coffee has long been a subject of controversy for humanity. King Charles II of England, Murad IV of the Ottoman Empire, and even Henry Ford have sought to banish coffee from their empires and enterprises, while Pope Clement VIII, Napoleon Bonaparte, and President John Adams championed the beverage. Today, the world consumes approximately one billion cups of coffee a day, yet few consumers have any knowledge about coffee other than where to buy it and how to brew it.

Those who roast coffee have an obligation to know more—for their own benefit and for those who might come to enjoy the product of their endeavors. Let's start at the beginning!

Coffee is the second-most widely traded commodity in the world. Petroleum is first, earning it the nickname "black gold," but truly, coffee is also black gold. There are more than 17 million coffee farmers, providing a means of sustenance for nearly a billion people worldwide. Americans alone consume 140 billion cups of coffee a year. How did this humble plant become such a dominant force in the world?

Today, the popular myth of Kaldi, the Ethiopian goatherd who "discovered" coffee circa 850 CE by observing the animated behavior of his goats when they chewed on the leaves and fruits of the coffee plant, is faithfully repeated everywhere as if it were historical truth.

Nobody knows the origin of this embellished myth. Goatherds populated the land for hundreds of years prior to that date, and coffee grew wild in the region throughout that time. It's doubtful it took hundreds of years for a wandering goat to suddenly discover that the fruit of the coffee bush was delicious and stimulating.

The earliest recorded knowledge and use of coffee was as a medicinal substance. Pictorial evidence on tablets as far back as 200 to 400 BCE shows that spiritual healers and medicine men used the leaves and fruit of the coffee plant in healing rituals. In the early centuries CE, it was recorded that Roman soldiers chewed on coffee fruit "jerky" for energy and sustenance before going into battle. Muslim texts state that the archangel Gabriel gave the first coffee bean to Muhammad (circa 600 CE) in order to provide him with healing powers, indicating that coffee's medicinal use was probably well recognized at that time.

Coffee Gets Roasted

While there is no reliable record of the first occasions of coffee roasting, methods popular in the early history of roasting and drinking coffee were primarily baking and fire roasting. After roasting, the beans were ground and generally boiled in a pot. Most of the roasting did not take place where the beans originated. The green, unroasted beans were carried far and wide. When Europeans entered the trade in the 16th century, beans were brought back from places of origin to processing plants in Europe by ocean-faring trade ships. Once the beans arrived in Europe, they were mostly stored green and were not roasted before being sold and brewed.

Consumers and coffee shops roasted their own coffee for hundreds of years. At the time, outside of the regions of origin, "green" coffee beans were actually typically white or pale yellow. This was due to "monsooning" that occurred

A vintage illustration depicting the leaves, flowers, and berries of Coffea (coffee plant). Additional coffee beans show both the whole bean and a cross-section.

A vintage engraving of people buying coffee from a coffee stall

during their sea voyage, when beans were stored in open holds and storehouses and exposed to wind, rain, extreme heat, and humidity. This caused the beans to swell with moisture, taking on a distinctive musty odor and taste profile, and changing color. Yet this aging also reduced many of the acids and bitterness of the coffee, and the overall profile was not objectionable. Monsooned coffee was the original coffee taste profile that the world outside of Africa was introduced to and became enamored of for centuries!

These pale, lower-density beans were typically pan roasted or fire roasted daily by a coffee shop purveyor before being ground and brewed for their customers. Consumers also took small paper sacks of green beans home to roast themselves, or made daily trips to a roaster who would sell roasted beans by the bag in small, premeasured volumes.

Coffee Conquers the Tropics Across the Globe

By the year 1610, the Dutch had created a worldwide coffee trade market. In 1696, the Dutch managed to either steal or cajole coffee plants from the Arabians and brought them to Indonesia. Once the beans were out of the bag, so to speak, plants were eventually carried to South America and the Caribbean along preestablished trade routes.

Coffee was identified as a cash crop by all the major colonial countries. Once separated from its origins, cultivation sprang up in more than 30 countries worldwide. Birds and mammals spread coffee even farther by defecating the seeds onto fertile lands at a distance from where they had eaten the tasty fruit. In this way, coffee skipped around the tropical regions of Africa and, later, the globe. It prospered at high altitudes in soils with boron and manganese, elements found in volcanic soils. To date, 125 distinct species of coffee have been catalogued, but

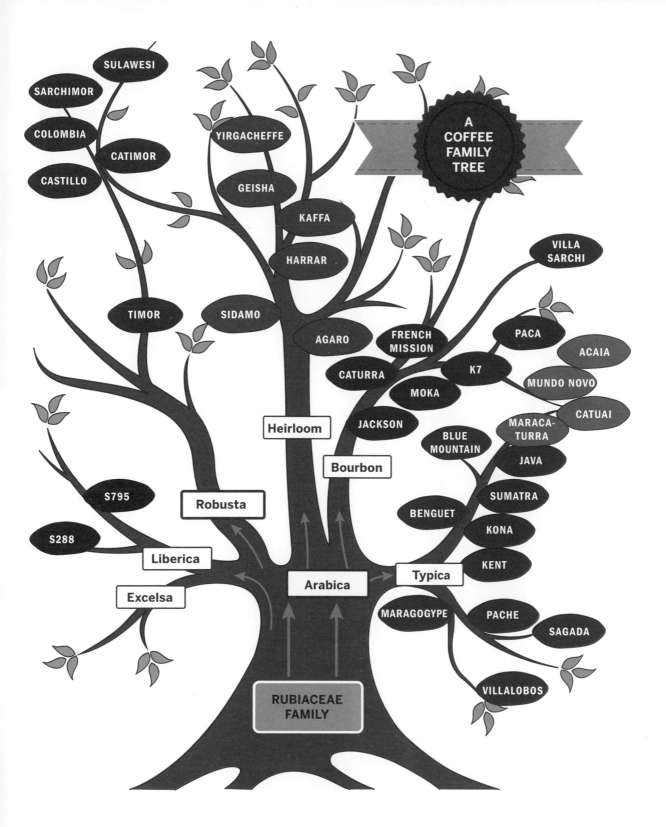

only four are common in commercial cultivation—Arabica, Robusta, Excelsa, and Liberica.

The most successful cultivations in terms of volume and trade opportunities occurred in four basic regions: Indonesia, Indochina, Brazil, and the Philippines. French Jesuits had created plantations throughout Indochina by the end of the 19th century (modern-day Cambodia, Laos, Myanmar, and Vietnam). Large plantations in Indonesia were created by the Dutch East India Company, while the Spanish brought coffee to the Philippines and the Caribbean. The Portuguese brought coffee to Brazil. At the same time, Puerto Rico became a successful cultivator. Their coffee was nicknamed "The Coffee of Popes and Kings" because it was of such high quality it made its way into many royal courts of Europe as well as the Vatican in Rome.

Coffee Species Origins

Genetically, coffee is highly adaptive to its environment, and natural mutations enable its spread and survival. The original Arabica species (*Coffea arabica L.*) and its subvarieties that were adopted by the Ethiopians and the Dutch were not in fact the earliest species to develop. The progenitor coffee species is now believed to be mostly similar to Robusta (*Coffea canephora*). *Coffea arabica L.* appears to be a hybrid between *Coffea canephora* and *Coffea eugenioides S*, a species that is grown in only a few locations, such as Sierra Leone. The original *Coffea canephora* developed on the middle of the East African coast, possibly in the lands that are now islands off the coast, such as Madagascar and Reunion, where Robusta varieties still predominate.

World's Top Coffee Producers

COUNTRY	VOLUME (METRIC TONS)	MOST COMMON SPECIES
Brazil	2,500,000	Arabica, Robusta
Vietnam	1,600,000	Robusta, Arabica, Excelsa
Colombia	800,000	Arabica
Indonesia	600,000	Arabica, Robusta
Ethiopia	380,000	Arabica
Honduras	350,000	Arabica
India	350,000	Arabica, Robusta
Uganda	290,000	Arabica, Robusta
Mexico	230,000	Arabica, Robusta
Guatemala	200,000	Arabica

Based on figures from 2018; weather and political events often change these rankings.

Coffee Today

Coffee as a commodity represents a unique opportunity for global change. It is a huge part of the global economy and creates an environmental impact across billions of acres of land. Today, the choices we make in growing, importing, roasting, brewing, and serving coffee have an enormous impact. Unlike many commodities, coffee has millions of small producers, and choices made on the individual level by growers and consumers can truly change the world for better or worse.

The following statistics about the world's top coffee producers show how coffee makes its way across the globe each year.

Who Drinks Coffee?

The answer may surprise you. For most high-volume requirements, small farmers simply cannot provide the volume and price needed. Larger plantations, often called factory farms, supply most high-volume requirements.

In the United States, 40 percent of coffee is consumed in government-run organizations or institutions including the military and prisons. This coffee is supplied in a bidding process and there is not often much concern paid to quality other than to ensure that the coffee is wholesome (free of contaminants, physically sound).

Another 35 percent of coffee (that typically does not meet Specialty Grade) is sold to suppliers of hotels and mass retailers.

About 15 percent is used for extracts or flavoring and not served as brewed coffee. This coffee is not Specialty Grade but usually is Grade B or other designation that indicates the coffee is of decent quality and taste.

Although Specialty Grade Coffee accounts for less than 10 percent of coffee consumed in the United States, it's this channel we focus on in terms of the welfare of small farmers due to the billions of dollars involved.

A coffee
plantation
near Manizales,
Colombia

Raw green coffee beans in a hopper, ready to be roasted

CHAPTER 2

THE GREEN COFFEE BEAN

Location and Cultivation

Coffee cultivation occurs across many types of landscapes, at varying altitudes, and may be as simple as handpicking coffee cherries from wild bushes in remote jungles or as involved as tilling and cultivating hundreds of acres in full sun on huge plantations.

When coffee grows in the wild, it typically follows routes in the forest where overhead growth does not block too much of the sun. It likes a good deal of direct sun, but because coffee easily dries out, locations where water gathers and the soil is porous are preferred. Because boron and manganese are needed for prolific growth, coffee prospers in mineral-rich volcanic soils.

The original Arabica varieties prospered in shaded areas, but coffee loves the sun. It also needs almost constant moisture in the soil, so it finds a compromise in nature—locations where the sun is strong but the soil is shaded enough to stay moist in dry months. Farmers who can irrigate coffee may want to produce it in direct sun for maximum growth, and they also may choose hybrids that are more resistant to drought. Full sun is an unnatural environment, and farms that cultivate on clear-cut land have reduced habitation for indigenous flora and fauna. Clear-cutting (removing all existing trees and vegetation) increases the fields' exposure to the elements and may create problems for the environment because of runoff. Contamination of ground soil can be caused by pesticide use and fertilizers.

Shade-Grown Coffee Versus Sun Grown

Shade-grown coffee seems like a great solution. When we hear the phrase "shade grown," we imagine lush jungles filled with wildlife where coffee grows naturally. But all it really means is the coffee meets the industry requirement for the term "shade grown" by experiencing a minimum of 20 percent shade. It also doesn't say anything about what types of plants are producing the shade. Farmers typically grow three layers of plants. The first layer is the coffee plant, the second layer is typically persimmon or another popular mid-growth plant with spreading leaves, and the top layer can be an avocado or nut tree. This provides multiple crops for the farmer and adds efficiency to the land use, but it is a totally unnatural environment for local fauna, who tend to shy away from these groves that offer few habitation opportunities.

THIS PAGE: Rolling hills covered in coffee and banana plantations near Buenavista, Antioquia, Colombia

OPPOSITE PAGE:
Top: A Rufous-collared sparrow. Bottom: A black and white Tegu lizard, one of many creatures that freely roam the forests of Brazil, including coffee plantations

THIS PAGE: A local farmer works the soil of a coffee plantation in Nicaragua

OPPOSITE PAGE: The sprawling hills of a Colombian coffee plantation

I have wandered the fields of coffee farms that use these shade-grown methods and not seen any wildlife. Then, in the evening, I've seen the hummingbirds and other small animals coming from quite a distance to feed on the farmhouse fruits and flowers.

In the Poços de Caldas in Minas Gerais, Brazil, some farmers use a different method. They create a checkerboard of farm plots among squares of preserved rainforest. By staggering these types of land in proper-sized lots, the wildlife resides close to the coffee plants and forages among them during the day. In rambling among the fields, I've observed dozens of bird species and small animals flying or wandering in and out of the coffee trees.

In order to know if a farmer is a good steward of the land, it is important to learn something about the grower of the coffee purchased and how they work with the environment. This will tell you more than a catchphrase.

Nurseries: Planting the Small Seedlings

Typically, seeds are sprouted and grown, or cuttings are created and rooted in small pots in protected areas. Clear plastic tarps overhead and on the sides protect against weather extremes. Nursery grounds tend to be stepped and flattened in layers to accommodate changes in level on the land, and irrigation channels or hoses supply water. Despite careful measures, nursery acres are susceptible to being wiped out by flooding or storm winds.

If the plants mature well, they are relocated to the fields and usually interspersed with other mature plants. It's not uncommon for small farmers to attempt to plant 20,000 seedlings per year. Coffee plants typically do not bear a productive amount of fruit until their third growing season.

A healthy coffee plant raised in a proper environment requires no chemical fertilizer or pesticide to prosper. Caffeine is a natural pesticide and most plants outgrow even destructive blights if they are strong enough.

Rows of Arabica
coffee plants in
a nursery

Fresh coffee cherries in different states:
whole, halved, and showing the mucilage
that houses the green coffee bean

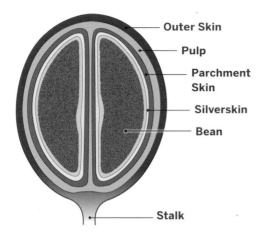

- Outer Skin
- Pulp
- Parchment Skin
- Silverskin
- Bean
- Stalk

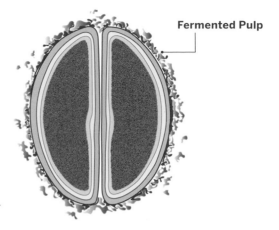

Fermented Pulp

What Is a Coffee Bean?

Coffee is a stone fruit, like cherries, plums, and peaches. The brightly colored fruit, called a coffee cherry, has an outer skin and juicy pulp. Beneath the pulp is a layer of sticky mucilage, a parchment layer, and a husk surrounding a stone, or seed. Usually, the seed splits in half during development, so each fruit has two seeds, each somewhat flattened from being pressed against the other. A small percentage of seeds do not split and are called peaberries because of their pealike shape and size.

As the plant is growing and maturing, it takes energy from the sun and pulls sap up through its roots into the leaves and fruit. When the sun sets, the plant exchanges sugars and other contents back into the soil while the fruit or leaves develop overnight.

Most coffee growing areas have wet and dry seasons. A few weeks into the dry season, the sugar content of the ripening fruit peaks as it is converted from starches stored in the fruit by the sap. The sugars in the fruit affect the flavor of the seed later on when the coffee is roasted. The more sugar, the more the coffee will "brown" and caramelize during roasting; this generally produces a richer flavor.

- Silverskin
- Mucilage

Initial Picking and Processing

The labor of picking is enormous. If the fruit is not picked promptly, it will over-ripen and rot.

Farmers who don't receive fair prices for their crops frequently recruit their own children to pick the crop—resulting in the children missing quite a bit of their educational development. Paying farmers fair prices for their crop can uplift an entire community; they are able to afford to pay temporary workers, and their children can remain in school.

Farmers who perform careful multiple pickings of the ripest cherries during the peak sugar season often create a "microlot" from these pickings. For these microlots, they may process the fruit differently, leaving some or all of the pulp and/or skins on the fruit during an initial drying and fermenting. This is called a "honey" process, and it enhances the sweetness and flavor of the beans.

THIS PAGE: Coffee beans left out to dry in the sun

OPPOSITE PAGE: Freshly picked coffee beans drying

If farmers are not drying the fruit themselves, the picked fruits are transported as quickly as possible to co-op or mill facilities. There, the whole crop is floated in water to separate the ripe from the unripe beans. The ripe beans sink, while the unripe beans mostly float and are skimmed off.

Processing cherries into beans requires separating the seeds from all other parts and drying them until they are stable for storage, transport, and roasting. The methods of accomplishing this task vary depending on the equipment available, the weather, and the desired taste profile.

What happens next depends on the curing method. In the "dry" or "natural" process, the cherries are carefully fermented for a number of hours and then laid out to dry in the sun. In the wet process, the cherry is washed to remove the fruit and pulp, then put into covered trays outdoors to dry. Kilns are

Cherries being spread out for natural drying process

used when the outdoor weather or facilities are insufficient for drying. Kiln-dried beans typically have less-developed flavor than sun-dried beans.

The beans must be stirred frequently to dry evenly. When they reach an optimal moisture content (typically about 11 percent), they are quickly bagged to stabilize their humidity. As soon as that batch of beans is safely bagged, a new batch is spread out to dry in a process that repeats many times until the entire harvest is complete.

At this stage, the beans still have their husk (commonly called "parchment"), which is a brittle coating that surrounds the beans. The parchment is removed from dried beans through pounding or milling. Once this outer layer has been removed from the beans, they finally look like the green coffee beans we know. These beans are loaded into canvas sacks and marked with information as to origin, brand, year, and other relevant information. Beans are stored in plastic sacks inside the canvas to withstand storage and transportation without picking up unwanted humidity. If you buy sacks of beans that have no inner moisture barrier, you should immediately repack the beans into airtight bags or bins.

Wet, Dry, or Honey: What Does It Mean?

The processing method has a significant impact on the coffee's final flavor profile. For example, because dry or naturally processed coffee spends a lot of time in contact with its pulp and skin, it absorbs the fruitiness and develops brown sugar and honey notes. It also has a stronger, fuller taste profile. On the other hand, washed coffee spends less time in its pulp and fruit, resulting in nutty, spiced, or chocolate tones.

WET OR WASHED PROCESSING

The cherries are run through a milling machine that slits the fruit and washes away the skin and the pulp, routing the beans with their mucilage and attached husk into a holding bin. The mucilage-covered beans resemble very large tomato seeds.

Most processing mills use huge pieces of machinery in a central location. However, smaller portable mills are now used by many small farmers who share the portable mill by towing it from farm to farm instead of transporting delicate, perishable fruits into town to the large mills. One portable mill may serve 2 to 10 farmers with adjacent plots of land.

DRY OR NATURAL PROCESSING

The beans, still inside the whole fruit, sit in a holding area for a certain number of hours and are then spread out to dry in the sun (if the weather cooperates). This takes longer than if the skin and pulp were removed first. During that extra time, the sugar and nutrients in the pulp and skin are absorbed into the beans and impart flavors and sweetness. Once the fruit dries, the beans are mechanically removed from the fruit. The naked beans are dried a second time, either in the sun or in a kiln.

PULPED OR HONEY PROCESSING

Using elements of wet and dry processing, beans are dried naturally with some of the pulp remaining on the hulls. This adds sugar to the beans, which translates into a more developed flavor profile with fruit and caramel notes.

HULLING

Hulling is the removing of the husks and parchment; it can be done in either wet or dry processes. Most coffee is dried

DRYING METHODS

There are many different methods of drying coffee fruits. Each imparts different flavors or qualities to the finished green beans. The choice of methods is often dictated by climate. Farmers may use any combination of the following steps as appropriate.

| **NATURAL SUN DRYING** | **WASHED, SUN-DRIED** | **WASHED, FERMENTED** |

1. Picked fruits are separated by hand to remove unripes and defectives.

1. Picked fruits are floated in water. The unripe beans float and are skimmed off.

1. Picked fruits are floated in water. The unripe beans float and are skimmed off.

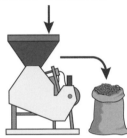

2. The fruits are spread on slabs under the sun and dried with the skins on.

2. The fruits are milled to remove the skins and washed to remove the pulp.

2. The fruits are fermented briefly to make it easier to remove the skins, and lengthen the time before they can be peeled. They are brought to a large mill, where they are peeled and washed.

3. The seeds, with their parchment, are dried on slabs or raised trays in the sun.

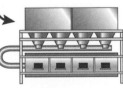

3. The seeds are kiln dried, then they go to be hulled.

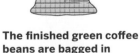

3. The dried fruits are run through a separator that removes the skins.

The seeds are dried and hulled to remove the parchment.

The seeds are dried to <12% moisture and graded for size.

The finished green coffee beans are bagged in canvas sacks.

with the parchment still on the bean in climates where the dry season brings reliable sunny weather for long periods. In wet climates, like Sumatra, it works better to wet-hull beans because they require less time overall in the sun to process into finished green beans. The parchment is removed before the beans have fully dried (typically when moisture is between 20 and 24 percent). The beans are then dried by machine or in the sun to about 12 percent moisture.

I mention these terms here because some origins, especially Indonesia, prominently state their hulling method. It's helpful to know that the wonderfully rich, earthy profile of wet-hulled coffee occurs when it is allowed to dry outdoors, because the sun bakes the flavor of the remaining pulp into the beans. This process generally produces a dark green, almost bluish bean, and there is often cracking at the tips due to the exposure of the wet inner bean to hot sun. But wet-hulled coffee dried indoors in heated drums will not have these flavor nuances.

Coffee Species

In North America we are continually bombarded with propaganda about Arabica beans being superior to all other varieties, particularly Robusta. It's probably safe to say that 99.9 percent of all coffee served in coffee shops in the United States is Arabica. That means that if you had a bad cup of coffee today, it was Arabica. If you had a great cup of coffee today, it was also Arabica. It's not the species alone that determines great taste but also the growing methods and altitude, the quality of processing, and how the coffee is brewed.

There are four commercial species of coffee that still survive to this day: Arabica (52 percent), Robusta (41 percent), Excelsa (6 percent), and Liberica (1 percent). Different species have unique advantages for cultivation in diverse environments, and each offers specific benefits in blends or in espresso, instant coffee, or extracts. All four species are delicious when well grown, properly processed, and served well. Although Excelsa and Liberica boast lower volumes, remember that the world produces tens of millions of tons of coffee a year, so even 7 percent is *a lot* of coffee.

The vast majority of the coffee produced worldwide is not intended for the discerning consumer. Less than 10 percent qualifies as specialty coffee. The rest is raised for extracts, instant coffee, sale to government institutions, and other less demanding markets.

Arabica is the most commonly grown coffee species, and it has the most subvarieties. Arabica has a high rate of adaptive mutation, and when these mutations produce something desirable, the mutation is named and line grown to produce a consistent lineage. Arabica is generally more delicate and prone to disease or failure in suboptimal conditions. This has led to extension modification of its genes, either by actual gene manipulation or by grafting another species into the line. As a result of considerably greater cultivation and manipulation, there is more reliably documented genetic and lineage information for Arabica than other species.

While **Robusta** gets a bad rap in North America (often referred to as tasting like "burnt rubber"), good Robusta is smooth and full of body and low in acid and bitterness. Its tarnished reputation is due to the tendency of United States coffee pundits and bloggers who have not tasted a top-quality highland Robusta to publish negative information about it. The myth of bad Robusta originated in the 1990s when Vietnam improperly cultivated Robusta and dumped it on the world market all at once in a shortsighted cash grab. North American coffee companies used the cheap coffee in their supermarket-brand coffee, resulting in it being difficult to find a decent cup of supermarket coffee. When coffee gourmets searched for a culprit responsible for this terrible coffee, they blamed the species rather than its improper cultivation.

A simple fact:
All the remaining four species of coffee can be grown under proper conditions so as to yield specialty coffee cupping scores. That is why they are still around!

After this debacle, Vietnam relearned how to cultivate decent coffee. The government allowed private vendors, such as Trung Nguyên and Highlands Coffee, to reestablish better methods of cultivation. Vietnam once again began to produce its share of Specialty Grade coffee. While most of Vietnam's Robusta is still what is called Exchange Grade, they also produce arguably the world's finest Robusta in their better growing areas.

A 2009 book written by an Italian coffee consultant exposed a surprising fact: The Italian espressos that had won about 80 percent of international competitions since 2005 contained top-quality, higher-altitude peaberry Robusta from the Dalat region of Vietnam. Soon after, most competitions began requiring that entrants label the coffee species in their blends. Many entries contained what they called "Asian Robusta," a euphemism for both Dalat Robusta and Robusta sourced from India.

Liberica is the rarest commercially cultivated coffee. It is incredibly important in coffee history and for its gene composition, so it should not be overlooked in a discussion about species. Liberica grows taller than other species and has natural resistance to coffee blight. Because of this, it replaced Arabica in the Philippines, Malaysia, and other locations during a worldwide coffee blight that occurred around 1890. Tremendously aromatic and rich, it has an earthy taste that some people find objectionable and others find sublime. It is called Barako Coffee in the Philippines, which translates two ways. Literally, a Barako is a fierce indigenous boar that populates Philippine forests. It is also a slang term meaning "studs" or "toughs," referring to sturdy sugarcane workers who were known to prefer this strong coffee.

Excelsa is thought to have developed from Liberica. It has an unusual aroma that does not appeal to some people, but its taste profile is so balanced and clean that it is used by master blenders to balance deficiencies in other beans.

It has an excellent cup profile, but its aroma prevents it from achieving wide popularity.

Understanding the Taste Palate and Why People Prefer Different Species and Profiles

Why does it seem so hard to agree on what great coffee actually tastes like? And why do some people prefer Arabica and some prefer Robusta? In order to understand what makes great-tasting coffee, there are two fundamental things to understand: 1) How the tasting apparatus (palate) works in humans, and 2) Why different species and varieties appeal to different palates. If you understand these things, you are on your way to becoming a master blender.

Keep the following definitions in mind as you read on:

Palate: Used in taste discussions two ways. The first literally refers to the roof of the mouth. The second refers to a person's tasting abilities and preferences.

Taste buds: Thousands of tiny sensors located on the complex surfaces of the tongue, lips, and back of the (literal) palate of the mouth and even down into the throat. The number of taste buds varies tremendously from person to person, depending on health, anatomy, and age. It is not unusual for there to be a five times differential in the number of taste buds between any two people; in rare cases, the ratio can approach 100 times.

Several studies performed and published by institutions in the United States, Canada, and Germany have documented the incredibly diverse palate sensitivities of humans.

A study performed by the University of Florida identifies three basic groups: 15 percent of the population belong to the "taste-impaired" group, 60 percent belong to the "normal tasters," and 25 percent are what they call "supertasters"—those whose taste buds can be so overwhelmed by a given taste that they may report experiencing something akin to pain. To complicate matters further, a person can be a supertaster for only certain taste sensations, such as sweet or bitter.

The soft palate is the tasting apparatus in humans that is partly present in the back of the (literal) palate; this area is also wired differently to the brain. Winemakers talk of the impression a wine has on the soft palate. This is an important consideration for coffee blenders as well. The front palate taste sensors respond best to acidity, aroma, and sweetness. These characteristics are strongest in Arabicas, so people who have "front palate" preference will enjoy a fine cup of Arabica and may find Robusta too bitter or flat. The soft (or back) palate responds to body and bitterness and retains memories of a taste experience better than the front palate. People with "back palate" preference find Arabica too thin and acidic, and they respond better to Robusta or Arabica/Robusta hybrids, such as Catimor and Timor.

In more than 10,000 blind taste tests I have performed, roughly half the testers prefer Arabica; the other half prefer Robusta. Moreover, a back-palate person who prefers a Robusta in a blind taste test will consistently pick back-palate coffees in further testing. They will avoid pure Arabica coffee unless it is a Robusta hybrid. They also tend to choose Liberica and Excelsa, which have taste profiles that are less specific to front or back palates. Armed with this information, how would you create an award-winning espresso? First, because the Specialty Coffee Association (SCA) and most cupping criteria were designed to evaluate Arabica, the deck is stacked in favor of front-palate coffee. If you want to score highly on standard points but also stand out with a unique, memorable profile, you could use a base of Arabica but include 20 percent Robusta and a touch of Excelsa

ANATOMY OF TASTE

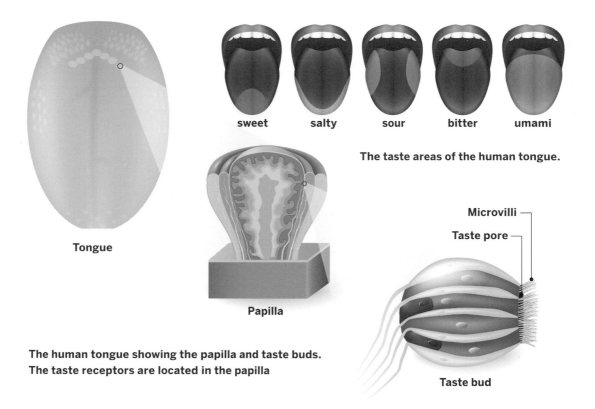

sweet   salty   sour   bitter   umami

The taste areas of the human tongue.

Tongue

Papilla

Microvilli

Taste pore

Taste bud

The human tongue showing the papilla and taste buds.
The taste receptors are located in the papilla

to supply any missing elements. This broadens the appeal to judges who are rating coffee based on Arabica profiles but typically have a critical 10 subjective points to award, based on how they personally enjoyed the taste profile. Despite their training, half of them might be back-palate people who respond well to a multispecies blend. That blended cup really might please everyone and get a few extra subjective points that can make the difference, since the winner is usually only one to three points above the rest of the field.

If you are not preparing a blend for entry in international competitions and just want to please yourself and friends, try a few experiments with different species or subspecies of

The human taste bud is a marvel of natural bio-engineering. Taste buds vary in number and sensitivity across different people and populations, probably reflecting natural migrations to and away from specific food sources

GREEN COFFEE COMPOSITION

Cellulose fiber	~33%
Oils/fats	~13%
Protein (aminos)	~11%
Sugars	~8%
Chlorogenic acid	~7%
Minerals	~4%
Caffeine	~1.5–2.5%
Trigonelline	~2%

ROASTED COFFEE COMPOSITION (MEDIUM ROAST)

Cellulose fiber	~33%
Oils/fats	~13%
Protein (aminos)	~9%
Sugars	~4%
Chlorogenic acid	~2%
Minerals	~4%
Caffeine	~1–2%
Trigonelline	~1%

beans to learn the taste preferences of your audience. The most important takeaway from learning about the diversity of the human palate is that it is unrealistic to think that any one coffee origin or species will please everybody and get universal acclaim as "the best coffee."

Coffee Chemistry

Coffee is one of the most complex foods on the planet. Experts claim that there are 400 to 1,000 or more compounds in coffee that affect taste. When we roast coffee, we are converting hundreds of these compounds into different compounds. Each of these conversions takes place at its own pace and temperature curve. Most of these conversions are beyond our influence, but some very pronounced flavor tones can be expressed or suppressed by roasting techniques.

The greatest changes occur in chlorogenic acid (which is responsible for much of the bitterness of coffee), proteins, sugars, caffeine, and trigonelline (a bitter alkaloid that is also responsible for much of the aroma in roasted Arabica). Robusta has less trigonelline and has double the caffeine of Arabica.

Selecting and Purchasing Green Beans

A decade ago, there were few places you could easily buy green coffee beans in small quantities in North America. As of this writing, the number of sources has increased exponentially. What criteria should you use for choosing?

PRICE

Oddly, price has little to do with quality. Price is generally driven by the origin species or variety and the volume the vendor is selling. You can pay a lot of money for a bland or unremarkable Arabica from an exotic-sounding locale, or get a bargain for a rich and satisfying bean from a pedestrian-sounding origin. Price is also affected by how many intermediaries your beans went through to get to you, since the price is marked up at every transaction.

Coffee math: The vendor selling you the beans has at least doubled their original purchasing price to cover overhead, labor, packaging, and other costs. For example, if you are buying a small quantity of beans for $5 per pound, the vendor will have paid no more than $2.50 per pound for them. Thirty cents of that price paid for shipping the beans via ocean freight, which brings the actual purchase price down to $2.20. If the beans were purchased from a broker or exchange, they would have taken at least 35 percent of that, bringing the price down to $1.43. Finally, subtract the cost to get the beans to port for shipping, bringing the original cost of the beans down to about $1.35 per pound.

For a farmer and their family to have a reasonable standard of living, they must sell their coffee for a minimum of $1.75 to $2.00 per pound. When you add in transportation, broker's fees, ocean freight, and vendor overhead, the final retail price is no lower than $7 per pound for small quantities.

High-volume buyers who buy beans that have been purchased in large quantities spend considerably less per pound: both markup and transportation costs are considerably lower. Pricing is totally different when you buy in large quantities

Beans for Roasting Newcomers

These are some bean suggestions that will serve a beginning roaster well.

Arabica successions that line up genetically in the Typica lineage are generally the easiest varieties to roast. They are usually graded for uniform size, and are generally of consistent density with fewer unripe beans than Robusta and other species. Brazilian and Central American Arabicas tend to have a wide range of desirable roast temperatures. Exceptions to this rule would be Sumatra and other Indonesian coffees. Arabicas that are successions from the Bourbon lineage are often more difficult to roast and require longer rest periods for evaluation and proper flavor development.

Catimor is a subspecies hybrid of Arabica and Robusta. For some reason, I have always had great luck with Catimor beans in any roaster, including my grill roaster that tends to produce uneven results in many bean types. Catimor always seems to have a desirable and even color and progresses very clearly through the cracking and development stages.

**Green coffee beans
stored in sacks**

because you are participating in a wholesale market channel. If the vendor buys in container volumes (7 to 15 tons) through Direct Trade with the farmer, your price might be as low as $3.00 to $3.50 for Arabica and still provide the farmer with the sought-after price of $1.75 or more. (Note that we are using rough prices based on an average market. Every year will be different, and the actual financial need of farmers is very dependent on their local economy and cost of living.)

Avoid buying small volumes unless you are sampling a new coffee. Look for 10-pound packages or whatever makes sense for your purposes and you should reduce your costs by at least 40 percent.

SOURCING COFFEE

When buying beans, you may see certifications such as "Rainforest Alliance Certified," "UTZ," or "Fair Trade." Some beans may indicate that the coffee production methods meet certain environmental or safe practice standards. Others, like "Fair Trade," indicate how the coffee is sold and purchased. Often certifications are printed on the canvas sack in which the coffee is transported in order to be visible to traders and purchasers. Other designations that may signify high quality or a particular processing style may also be printed on the sack (e.g., Organic, Triple-Picked, Wet-Hulled, Natural). It's important to understand what these certifications mean.

SAMPLE RANGE OF PRICING

Farmer's production cost: $0.80 per pound for coffee cherries; $1.10 for finished beans

Broker pays: $1.00 to $1.50, depending on market

Co-op pays: $1.20 to $1.70, depending on market and region

Fair Trade pays: $1.20 to $1.80, depending on market

Direct Trade pays: $1.50 to $3.00 or more

(PRICING BASED ON A CENTRAL AMERICAN AVERAGE; IT WILL VARY AROUND THE WORLD.)

BROKER PURCHASED

Co-ops, brokers, and intermediaries purchase unprocessed coffee berries from farmers at the lowest possible market price, then hull, dry, store, and resell the beans themselves. Farmers make little profit and may even post a loss in a year when market prices are falling.

FAIR-TRADE CERTIFIED

Fair Trade is a private enterprise that enrolls farmers in a program that promises them a margin above market cost and better working conditions. However, the Fair-Trade price is typically only $0.20 higher per pound than the broker's prices, and farmers must pay to enroll in the program.

DIRECT TRADE

In Direct Trade, farmers must either process the beans themselves or pay a local mill for processing. If the mill is operated by brokers or a co-op, farmers can sell the beans to the mill. Farmers who sell through Direct Trade to an end buyer get the best possible price for their beans; this is always the preferred option. However, the farmer may have no way to accomplish this.

ORGANIC COFFEE

While the concept of organic food sounds wonderful, the reality is far murkier. Before a farmer can claim they are "certified organic," they must invest three years and pay a certification fee of at least $3,000 (plus yearly inspection fees). This is impossible for most small farms. The difficulty of tracing any specific coffee bean to the exact field where it grew makes it difficult to verify claims that a bean was organically grown. Farmers who do manage to get the certification often save money by certifying only one of their plots of land—and then

use that certification to sell *everything* they produce. Sometimes they even purchase their neighbors' crops and resell them as their own to get the higher organic pricing.

It is rare to find properly maintained organic farms selling exclusively their own organic produce. Only trust "organic" if you can see the traceability and are sure it is for real. Many people mistakenly believe that US Customs or the FDA are involved in testing incoming food sources to see if they are organic or not. This is wrong; they do not test at the point of entry.

Even worse, the high costs of producing certified organic coffee often forces the farmers to cut corners elsewhere. Being organic does *not* make a coffee tastier. In fact, because the farmer spent their limited budget on expensive certification fees instead of using it to maximize coffee quality, the opposite is often true.

The best way to ensure your purchase is environmentally sound is to buy coffee that can be traced to a specific farm or group of farms that uses safe and sustainable agricultural practices. This is another way in which Direct Trade helps both you and the farmers. Traceability creates accountability. It also creates pride for the farmer by giving them a valuable reputation to build and protect. If you want your coffee consumption to be ethical, buy 100 percent Direct Trade coffees from vendors and farmers who care about safe and sustainable agriculture.

Sourcing Coffee Responsibly

Every bean should have a story. When you see green beans for sale that list only the origin region, you can't know how those beans are sourced and you should avoid them. Buy from vendors who can tell you which farms or co-ops provided the beans and look for the terms under which they were bought and the ethics of the growers. For example, *"These beans were grown on Megatoro Estate in the Ruiru Constituency in Kiambu County, Kenya, and purchased in Direct Trade by us. The Estate provides workers with training opportunities, a health clinic, and on-site schooling for children."* It also helps if pictures and other specifics are presented.

In some countries, the majority of labor is provided by workers who toil in inhumane conditions for substandard wages, with no access to health care or education for children. Most of these abuses occur on large "factory" farms that supply the world's largest coffee retailers. Buying beans from smaller farmers or co-ops that do not exploit their members can often guarantee that better conditions exist for the growers and laborers.

Environmental considerations are also important. Production methods should have low environmental impact and high sustainability.

HERE ARE SOME OF THE MAIN ETHICAL CONSIDERATIONS TO WATCH FOR:

Purchasing method: Beans purchased under Direct Trade, Contract-Grown, and Fair-Trade terms, or purchased from member-owned-and-operated co-ops can usually assure you that the growers and laborers are being treated fairly.

Production method: Manual harvesting, shade growing or interspersing with conservation land, Rainforest Alliance, Safe & Sustainable Agriculture, and UTZ-Certified Good are designations that indicate care for the environment. "Organic" is a certification often used misleadingly when it comes to coffee and is not reliable.

Traceability: Blockchain data tracking and technology, such as Radio Frequency ID Tags, are increasingly being used to verify food producers, practices, and accountability. If such data is not available, be sure you trust the vendor from whom you purchase to provide reliable information.

Always remember that coffee is the second-most valuable commodity traded across the world. When sourced ethically, it has tremendous potential to change the world for the better. Your actions matter!

THIS PAGE: Three men in Colombia transporting sacks of coffee

OPPOSITE PAGE: Sacks of Colombian coffee

A variety of coffee samples ready for tasting

Single Varieties and Single-Origin Coffees Versus Blends

Single-origin coffees are great fun, allowing you to experience specific unique terroirs and taste profiles. But, as we previously learned, different varieties of coffee stimulate different areas of the human palate. Just as no single instrument can play a symphony, no single coffee can hit every flavor note. You will find the greatest satisfaction by blending two or more varieties of coffee to create a full orchestra.

Varieties are divisions within species. Cats and dogs are different species, but both are mammals. A poodle and a Great Dane are both species of dog, but they are quite different genetically. Arabica and Robusta are different species, but both are coffee. Within the Arabica species, there are subspecies, or varieties, such as Bourbon, Typica, Catuai, and more. They have the main characteristics of Arabica in bean shape, and plant and leaf structure, but have important variations, such as fruit color and taste. A single farm may grow only the Arabica species, but they typically grow more than one variety.

A good example of how blending works in food is apple pie. When you go apple picking, you see that farmers usually grow many varieties of apples. A good, balanced apple pie might contain Cortland, McIntosh, and Granny Smith apples. Each apple contributes something valuable to the taste and body. In coffee blending, you may combine a fruity coffee, a sweet coffee, and one with a darker profile for similar reasons—breadth and balance.

All the top-selling coffee brands in the world are blends of at least three origins with a variety of genes. The companies choose multiple origins and try to balance different species and varieties for best overall flavor. Remember how palates work. If you don't cover more than one base with your coffee, you will not get the most satisfaction. You may be more successful blending multiple species and varieties of beans than using just one origin and variety. Experiment with blending until you learn how to balance blends for specific flavors and profiles that please you, your friends, and your customers.

Coffee beans mid-roast in
a large industrial roaster

PART II: THE ROASTING PROCESS AND EQUIPMENT

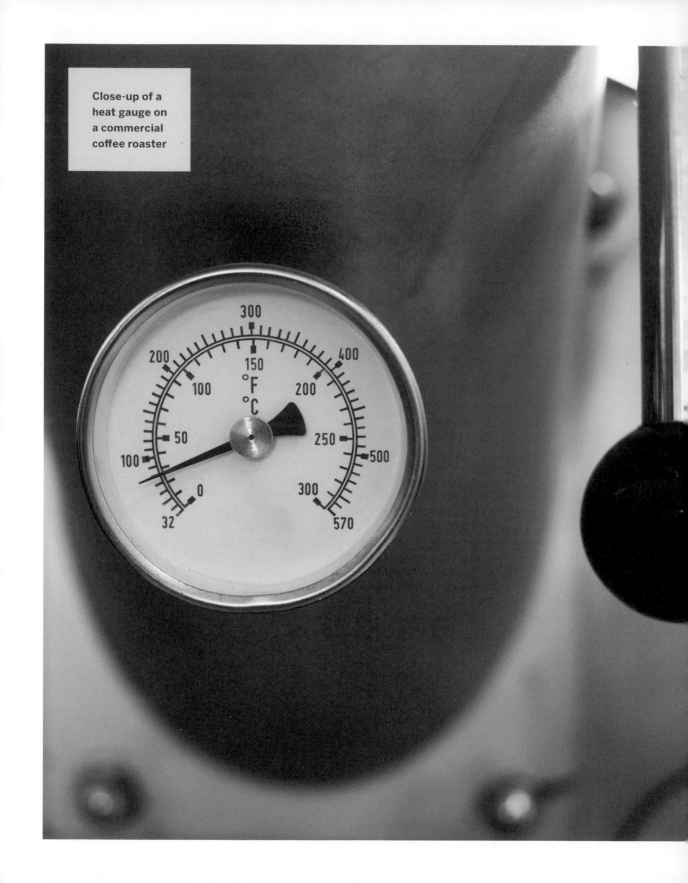

Close-up of a heat gauge on a commercial coffee roaster

CHAPTER 3
ROASTING EQUIPMENT

Applying Heat to Beans

In its simplest definition, roasting means applying heat to green coffee beans to convert them into a brewable form that is familiar to us. The basic objective is to bring about the conversion of hundreds of compounds that create the coffee taste we are looking for. Because the ultimate product of roasting can be used for an assortment of purposes, such as making instant coffee, extract, or espresso, brewing methods—options for machinery and processes—can vary, depending on your desired outcome.

The volume of roasting also affects the choice of method. If the roaster is happy producing three or four ounces at a time for personal consumption, the choices are pretty much unlimited. But if the objective is to produce three tons of roasted coffee beans a day for a commercial packing company, the options narrow and the roaster needs to select carefully the appropriate machinery and method.

To some degree, the roasting volume dictates available options. If you want to roast primarily for yourself, there is little concern about volume, so you can choose based on options such as cost, size, convenience, ventilation, and time it takes to roast a batch. If you want to share your roasting and blending efforts with family and friends, you need to skip past the methods that are limited to three to five ounces per 20 minutes and consider methods that let you produce at least a couple of pounds an hour. If you

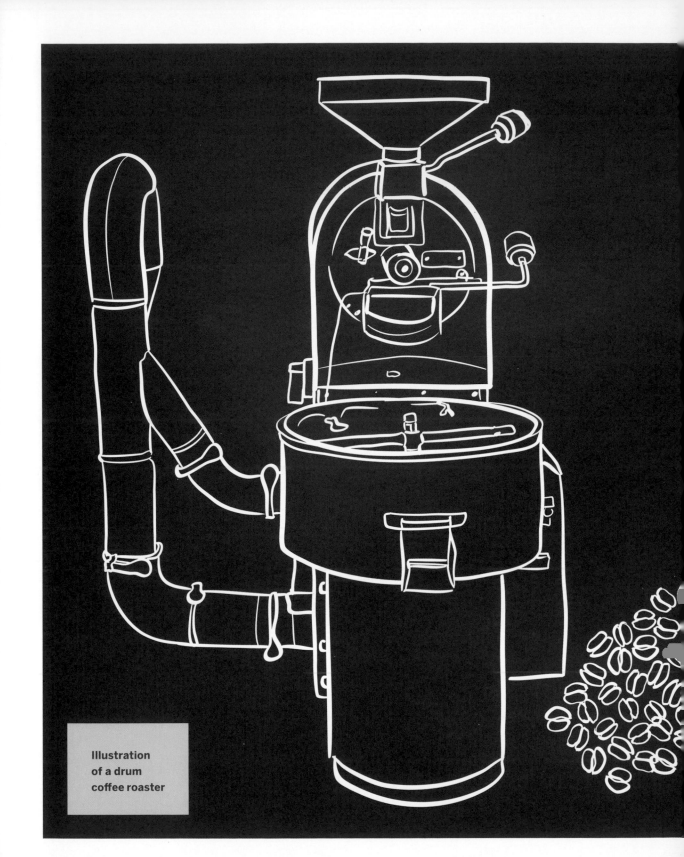

Illustration of a drum coffee roaster

are starting a coffee shop, you need to look at options that will produce at least three to five pounds per batch. The way heat is applied and the speed of the roast drastically affect your end product. Once you choose equipment appropriate for the desired volume, you need to compare the methods in which the heat is applied to the beans. To achieve good results, roasting equipment must conform to the basic parameters of a proper roasting heat curve. Some machines use mostly air convection, some use primarily radiant heat, and most use some combination of the two. In the end, the biggest concerns are simple: creating the taste we desire in a useful volume. These objectives ultimately guide our choices.

Commercial Roasting/ Large Volume Equipment

There are two basic roasting methods that commercial roasters use. In the first, a rotating drum circulates beans so that they are subject to both radiant heat from the heating source and convection air currents. The second relies on suspending the beans in a spinning airstream or vortex. The air suspension method uses almost entirely highly heated, hot-air convection for roasting. A good comparison is a home oven, which can use both radiant heat and convection to cook. When you broil something, you put the food near the top burner, and the cooking is performed almost entirely by direct heat from the heating source. This is radiant heat. When you bake, food is placed in the middle of the oven; because the heat comes from a faraway source, you are relying on circulating air to do most of the cooking. That is convection.

PROFESSIONAL ROASTERS

Commercial Drum Roaster

Centrifugal Roaster

Fluid-Bed Roaster

DRUM ROASTERS

Drum roasters can be any size. The drum can be as small as a coffee can, as big as a barrel, or even the size of a cement mixer. Drum roasters tumble the beans, usually at a speed of 30 to 60 rotations per minute, to ensure even heating. Some look like a rotisserie and have been crafted based on that principle. This method relies more or less equally on radiant (often called conductive) heat and convection. The operator can balance radiant and convection heat during the process by adjusting the airflow or heating element settings. The heat source might be quartz filaments at the back of the machine or a gas flame in the bottom of the roasting chamber.

Drum roasters that can produce 10 to 30 pounds per hour are common in small roasteries and coffee shops in North America. The Oro 10-pound roaster has a gas flame grid in the bed, a rotating drum, and an adjustable airflow. The roaster mostly uses convection when the airflow volume is up; when the air volume is set low, the heat is mostly radiant from the gas flame. Commercial drum roasters are capable of roasting thousands of pounds per hour; their operation is fundamentally the same as that of the smaller drum roasters, just implemented on a larger scale.

FLUID/AIR AND PACKED-BED ROASTERS

Another method for circulating the beans without using a rotating drum is to force air up through a bed with holes or a wire grid. When the force of the air is strong enough, the beans float on the air, bumping into one another, the bed, and the sides of the roasting chamber.

Packed-bed roasters are considered obsolete because they do not provide even distribution of heat. However, you will still see them listed under "roaster types."

Image of a commercial drum roaster

Fluid-bed roasters use a roasting chamber with a gridded or screened bed through which air can flow. They are called "fluid bed" because they do not have a solid bed. Within the processing industry for other products, fluids are often used to circulate the particles, although in coffee roasting, air is used. There are many styles of fluid-bed roasters; a popular design for these is a tall tapered cylinder, with the narrow end at the bottom. The airflow is often directional, causing the beans to swirl in a circular pattern. Others simply blow air straight up like a corn popper, and they have controls to manage the loft of the beans.

There are some issues with fluid-bed roasters:

1. If the beans are not evenly graded, the smaller beans will loft and roast differently.

2. As the beans get drier, they loft higher, reducing the convection heat transfer and making adjustments necessary.

VORTEX-STYLE AIR ROASTERS

Vortex-style air roasters create a swirling motion, like a tornado, which tends to homogenize the bean loft and motion, reducing some of the loft issues. They apply the airstream in one direction at all times.

CENTRIFUGAL ROASTERS

Centrifugal roasters are essentially air convection, fluid-bed roasters, but they add a spinner on the bed, creating the same effect as the vortex blower. These are often large machines that can handle thousands of pounds per hour. They are fully convectional in heating.

TANGENTIAL ROASTERS

Tangential roasters are unique in that they circulate the beans mechanically with paddles or blades while blowing heated air through them. This enables both radiant and convection heating, and also integrates the exothermic process in which the beans radiate their own heat, because they are not subject to extreme air convection.

Small-Volume/Home Roasters

We see many of the principles used in commercial roasters at work in small home roasters.

SMALL-DRUM ROASTERS

There are many brands of small-drum roasters available as countertop-style devices or for outdoor use, including open-fire roasting and barbecue grill roasting. There are hundreds of videos on the Internet of DIY drum roasters and rotisseries that have been jury-rigged by inventors and innovators. They can roast from 8 ounces up to about 20 pounds. The drum might actually be a can with holes drilled in it, or it might be a stainless-steel wire mesh cage.

Drum machines are usually more expensive than simple air convection machines, so most people choose an air convection machine or a hot-plate stirrer (like a Whirley Pop) when they first purchase a home roasting machine. However, small-drum roasters tend to produce a more even roast with more control of the process.

An example of a popular home roasting machine is the Behmor 1600. It has quartz heating elements in the back, a rotating drum, and a fan to circulate air inside the roasting chamber.

Behmor Home Drum Roaster

Whirley Pop popcorn maker

Roasting over an open fire

VINTAGE ROASTERS: Before the advent of modern coffee roasting technology, coffee roasters had to manipulate their equipment by hand to get an optimal batch of roasted coffee

Advantages: This roughly $400 machine is fully programmable and can roast up to a pound of coffee in a light or medium roast (8 to 12 ounces in darker roasts) in an average 20-minute roasting cycle. This style of roaster usually has some smoke suppression and can be used indoors next to an open window with good ventilation or on a back porch. Roast results are highly reproducible using the same programmed settings.

Disadvantage: The cooldown is slow because the beans cannot easily be taken from the drum until the entire machine has cooled.

GRILL ROASTERS

These are typically drum machines that operate like a rotisserie. They are mounted on a stock propane-driven barbecue grill and run by an exterior motor. The grill provides the flame heat source and the motor keeps the beans circulating, typically at 60 revolutions per minute.

Advantages: Equipment cost is very low for a large capacity of beans in each batch (typically 3 to 20 pounds). A large amount of natural ambient air leakage takes place, but it's easy to balance the heat from the flame source versus the loss from convection to the outside. The lid can be raised or lowered to adjust the amount of convection and smoke retention.

Disadvantages: Roasting requires a huge amount of fresh air intake and gives off a lot of smoke, so it must be performed outdoors. It is also difficult to get even distribution of heat across the drum cage. In a large roasting, it's common to have a variance of up to 20 degrees or more from one side to the other, which can be a serious problem for achieving specific desired results. Because results are not reproducible, keeping records is largely futile. Sound and appearance are the main ways to gauge your roasts.

CAMPFIRE ROASTERS

These are typically rotisseries with a motor driver or hand crank and are crudely positioned on rocks or bricks and turned until the beans are done.

Advantages: The cost is low for roasting high volumes. If you like smoky, fire-roasted taste profiles, this method produces some very stunning profiles.

Disadvantages: You are very likely to burn yourself or the beans. The only way to control the temperature and roast process is to keep an eye on it and listen for cracking. Also, after the roasting is done, the hot beans need to be transported to a cooling device or area. This is not a safe or sane method for most people!

AIR-POPPER-STYLE ROASTERS

Many beginners use an actual hot-air corn-popping machine to roast coffee beans. These machines are typically inexpensive but have few safeguards against overheating, and blow chaff and smoke everywhere. I do not recommend buying any air-popping machine that is not specifically designed to accommodate coffee bean roasting.

There's a plethora of air-roasting machines built on a similar principle to that of the basic corn popper. These machines add capacity and safeguards, and some have coffee-roasting-specific features, such as chaff collectors. Prices of machines that improve on the basic corn popper start around $70 and can go up to $1,000 or more.

An improved corn popper, such as a 1500-Watt West Bend Poppery, has a better airflow angle, has a larger bed and heater than most corn poppers, and is commonly used for roasting coffee.

A Fresh Roast SR800 Roaster is a professional-quality machine that was specifically designed for roasting coffee.

Air popper

It uses a similar hot-air method. It handles about 4 ounces of green beans, has a couple of heat settings, and boasts a fan-only cooling function. It also has a chaff collection basket.

Advantages: Enhanced air-popping-style machines can be simple to operate and cover the basics. Some provide a fair amount of temperature control and let you change your roasting times by adjusting temperature up and down.

Disadvantages: Decent air-pop machines may be half the cost of a small-drum roaster, but they are nowhere near as adjustable or capable of reproducible results. If you are considering spending more than $100 on a machine, it is advisable to spend a little more and purchase a roaster that allows more control and has a higher roast capacity.

PAN FRYING

Pan frying is the earliest method of roasting coffee, practiced since at least the 15th century. Until commercially packed coffees became available around 1910, most Americans pan-roasted coffee at home. They either stirred the beans in a pot on the range top or baked the beans in a pan in the oven. Manufacturers of the era were creative in addressing this problem: They created cast-iron pans that had hand cranks and even belts that connected to record players or motors! Coffee roasted this way is usually inferior, since it is hard to apply uniform heat in a proper roasting curve, and it is very difficult to turn the beans evenly to ensure consistent roasting on both sides.

The Whirley Pop, which has been around since the 1980s, is a modern take on the crank-turning cast-iron pan. While it is an improvement over traditional pan frying, it still requires a lot of manual attention to get even results.

Advantages: Pan frying is cheap, easy, and relatively safe, since the beans can be easily handled after roasting, dumped

Coffee beans roasting over a fire in Indonesia

into a sieve, or spread out to cool with a fan. You can also add flavorings or butter oil to jazz up your coffee. More than four ounces of beans can be roasted at a time, although the amount depends on how much effort you want to put into stirring and how long you are willing to wait for the roast.

Disadvantages: It's difficult to get a totally even roast. The variables of heat and stirring times mean your roast isn't reproducible. This method also requires a well-ventilated area, either outdoors or under a professional, chef-style ventilation hood.

MECHANIZED PAN ROASTERS

Mechanized pan roasters are essentially pans with their own heat source and stirrers run by an electric motor. The cost for a reliable machine starts at around $120 and will do a fairly consistent roasting job in comparison to hand-crank machines.

Advantages: It requires no manual stirring, offers some heat setting options, and creates fairly consistent results.

Disadvantages: It's awkward to get the beans out of the roasting pan, and the beans don't turn as well as with other methods, such as air roasting and drum roasting. It's hard to get superior results.

Mechanized pan roaster

Recommendations

Most novice coffee roasters tire quickly of hand-stirring and turning methods and get discouraged by inconsistent results. It's unlikely that you'll want to share inconsistent or bad roasts with others, and it's infeasible to expect to sell such results. Buyers and consumers expect consistent high quality from fresh, hand-roasted coffee. If your beans are not evenly roasted or suffer from the faults that commonly occur in manually turned beans, it's unlikely that your coffee will be pleasing or result in repeat sales.

While you might initially want to play with the Whirley Pop or corn popper, if you want to progress with your roasting endeavors, you should ultimately settle on a more expensive machine that offers consistency and higher volume.

My choice for a small roaster that can roast up to 12 ounces of dark roast coffee is the Behmor 1600, a proven small-drum roaster. I use the Behmor for research and development, finding that results achieved in the Behmor usually translate and scale up when I use larger drum roasters. If $400 is too high for a starting machine, consider an air popper like the Fresh Roast SR800 (~$260), which can handle up to 8 ounces and provides fairly reproducible results by using consistent weights of beans, temperature setting, and a timer.

Equipment Used to Monitor Commercial Roasting

If you are a home roaster with small equipment, your options for controls and monitoring are limited. However, understanding the purpose of this equipment can guide your understanding of the roast process. The following discussion will focus on the two most common types of roasting: drum and fluid bed (remember, fluid-bed coffee bean roasters do not actually use liquids; they use air).

Many roasting machines have a gauge that shows the relative strength of the gas flame or electric heating element, like the dial on a stovetop that reads Low–Medium–High or is calibrated on a number scale. This is more intuitively useful than displaying the actual temperature of the flame or heating element. Knowing the exact temperature of the heating element sounds great, but in practice, it's deceptive. The amount of heat reaching the beans depends on too many factors. Only measuring the temperatures in the roasting chamber will give you this crucial information.

THERMOMETERS/PROBES

Accurate, quick temperature readings are critical to commercial roasting. Typically, probes are used to monitor temperature.

The location of temperature probes will alter the results of your temperature readings. Different machines will have different heat distributions, skewing temperature readouts higher or lower depending on their design. Thus, one machine might read 440°F, while another reads 445°F for the same roast level. Similarly, different probes may offer slightly different results on different machines. Fortunately, the amount of skew is usually consistent, so if you are transferring from one machine to the other, just consistently adjust by the same amount.

Resistance Temperature Detector (RTD) probes are very accurate and durable and protected by a stainless-steel sheath, but they are also expensive. Thermocouples are a little less accurate and more fragile but less expensive. It is important to use an RTD probe when measuring in any location where the probe could be damaged, such as inside the drum of a drum roaster. Measuring ambient air temperature is less demanding, so if the budget is tight, a thermocouple is okay to use there.

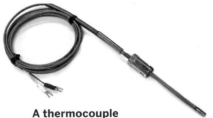

A thermocouple temperature probe

DRUM ROASTER TEMPERATURE MONITORING

In drum roasters, two measurements are generally taken: one from the middle of the beans to measure their internal temperature and one from the air outside the beans to measure the ambient temperature in the roasting chamber. The beans' internal temperature lets us plot their roasting curve and tells us when the beans are done. The ambient air temperature monitors how much heat is being applied to the beans via convection.

Manufacturers and users argue about the accuracy of probes placed within the bean flow of different brands and styles of machines. It is not uncommon to have to take results from one machine and lower your numbers by 5°F or more for

Arabica coffee beans released from the roaster and onto a cooling bed

another machine. For example, if you achieve one color and taste result on one machine at a bean temperature reading of 440°F, you might find that you would look for an internal temperature of 445°F on another machine using a different probe type or location.

Typically, having two probes is sufficient to achieve roasting curve results, as it allows you to monitor the rise of the internal bean temperature and adjust the ambient air temperature so it stays where you want it.

A drum roaster is likely to have an RTD probe for the bean temperature. The ambient air sensor might be a similar probe or might use a thermocouple. The thermocouple gets its reading from electrical variances that occur when two opposing metals create an electrical current upon heating. Thermocouples are more prone to damage, so they are not typically used in the bean flow.

FLUID-BED ROASTER TEMPERATURE MONITORING

Because the beans inside a fluid-bed roaster are "floating" on air, it is difficult to place a probe where it will measure the internal temperature of the beans the way it can in a drum roaster. Only the air temperature can be reliably measured. Doing this accurately requires two or more probes placed in different locations within the airflow.

A good deal of calculating needs to be done between the available probes to deduce the correct temperature of the beans themselves. Thus, temperature control in a typical fluid-bed roaster is less precise than in a drum roaster. To compensate, the roast operator uses timing of the roast and programs to create similar roasting times and curves. Keeping a detailed log is vital. Once a desired result is obtained, the next roast for that profile will simply duplicate the source temperature, weight of beans, and airflow. Adjustments can be made spontaneously to compensate for differences in bean mass, ambient temperature outside the roaster, and other variables.

MONITORING TEMPERATURE INSIDE SMALL HOME ROASTERS

Many small roasters do not display the temperature of beans or the air in the roasting chamber. Built-in temperature measurement capabilities are limited: Small drum roasters will have an air temperature sensor to help the machine keep the air at a certain temperature by automatically turning the heating element up or down, and some air poppers have a safety cutoff that is triggered if the unit gets too hot. Some do-it-yourselfers manage to mount probes inside their roasters, but they still have the basic temperature control limitations of a small roaster.

KEEPING LOGS

Truly professional roasting methods rely on logging results to create profiles that can be reproduced over and over. Logging can be as simple as jotting notations in a notebook or as complex as creating a complete operations log on a computer. Different operators can get similar results on similar machines when they exchange logs with one another. A saved log can give an operator a starting point for a roast. After matching the log and examining the results, the operator can make educated adjustments.

SAMPLE OPERATIONS LOG

BEAN	WEIGHT	TIME	TURN-AROUND TEMP	TURN-AROUND TIME	TEMP/ DIFFERENTIAL AT FIRST CRACK
Jampit	10 lb	12 min	170°F	1.0 min	387°F/80°F
D. Bourbon	10 lb	14 min	165°F	1.1 min	392°F/70°F

For small-machine operators, logging might simply be a matter of recording certain parameters in a grid:

The simple data on pages 66 and 67 is enough to ensure a consistent result every time. Occasionally, differences in environmental variables may require adjustments. For example, when roasting in cold weather, the operator might compensate for the cold by raising the flame 5 percent in order to ensure beans reach the desired temperature at the desired time.

COFFEE REFRACTOMETERS

A coffee refractometer is a device that is relatively new in the world of coffee roasting and brewing; it provides a way to measure the total solids in brewed coffee. Refractometers measure density and porosity—more solids mean more body. A roaster might change the roasting profile or program to achieve more or less density if the expected results were not achieved. To use a refractometer, you must always brew coffee in the exact same way so that results will be comparable (e.g., 20 grams of ground coffee with a grinder setting of Fine Drip in a 12-ounce press with a three-minute brew time and a water temperature of 203°F). Most home roasters simply rely on taste, as refractometers are expensive and are usually measuring subtleties beyond their ability to actually control.

Refractometer

SAMPLE OPERATIONS LOG (CONTINUED)

DEVELOPMENT TIME	DEVELOPMENT AIR TEMP	DEVELOPMENT AIRFLOW	SECOND CRACK	DUMP TEMP
2.7 min	455°F	7	442°F	445°F
4 min	445°F	7	440°F	443°F

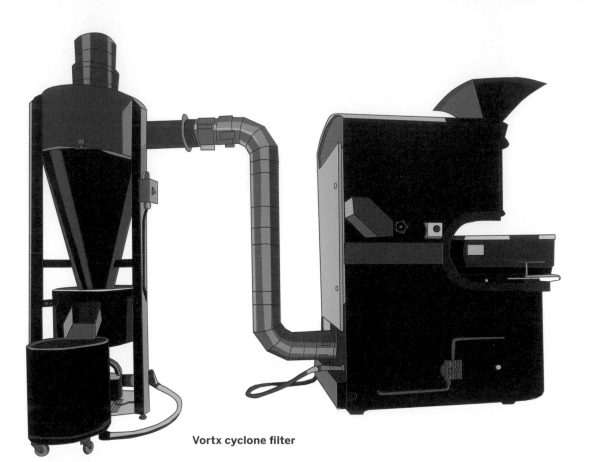

Vortx cyclone filter

Afterburner

AFTERBURNERS/POLLUTION CONTROL

Coffee roasting creates fumes and smoke; if roasting occurs in volume in a setting close to other homes or businesses, it becomes important to use smoke suppression and other controls to alleviate air pollution. Some roasters are equipped with catalytic converters that use a redox reaction to oxidize and absorb particles and fumes. Afterburners superheat the exhaust from the roaster, which carbonizes most of the particulate and breaks down fumes.

There are also smoke suppression systems that rely on ionization and filters to trap ionized particles. These are less expensive than afterburners and often reduce enough exhaust to satisfy local clean-air requirements. Small roasting machines sometimes have an ionizer or other slight smoke

suppression system to reduce the smoke, but they are usually only partly effective.

If you want to roast indoors, you should definitely look for a unit that says it has smoke suppression, and you will still need very good ventilation to the outside. If you have a high-quality ventilation hood in your kitchen, use that. If not, set up beside an open window and use a small fan to gently blow the smoke out the window.

Enveloped in smoke, freshly roasted beans are released into a cooling tray before being packaged or ground

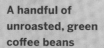

A handful of
unroasted, green
coffee beans

CHAPTER 4
PREPPING FOR THE ROAST

Healthy, Sound Green Beans

Green coffee beans are a natural food. Like all natural foods, they need to be checked for cleanliness and condition. If you have purchased good-quality beans, most of this checking and selection has been done before you purchased them, but I always examine my green beans and recommend that you do the same. It's a good habit, and every now and then I find a pebble or other random undesirable that slipped through, even in the highest-quality beans.

Bean colors can range from a yellowish cream to various shades of gray-green to dark brown. There may or may not be a reddish or yellowish coating of dried pulp attached to the beans. There may be no visible chaff (the thin, paperlike coating on the beans) or quite a bit of chaff, especially in the fold of the bean. There can be a lot of variance in the appearance of the beans. Variations in appearance are not inherently an indication of poor quality; some types of coffee are naturally less homogenous than others. For instance, some naturally dried Excelsa beans have a reddish hue and others have a dark green hue (this is common; I like to call them "Christmas Tree Beans").

Generally, naturally dried beans and high-altitude beans tend to be a darker green than other beans. This represents a density of the bean, and usually higher chlorophyll, which results in stronger taste. But color is never really a fully reliable measure of bean quality.

A well-processed Arabica bean will usually be clean and sound, with few broken or discolored beans mixed in and not too much chaff or pulp. You should expect exceptions only in special cases, such as a rare species (which may hold chaff tightly in its folds) or honey-process beans (in which the pulp usually stains the beans).

Defective Beans

Because coffee beans are a natural food product, a small number of defects is expected. Most "defects" are still perfectly healthy to use, particularly if only the occasional bean is defective. Specialty Grade 1 coffee is defined as beans that contain fewer than three full defects per 350 grams of beans. Generally speaking, defective beans are removed to improve the taste, not because they are unhealthy or dangerous.

The following are examples of the different kinds of defects you can find in your beans. You can choose for yourself how stringent you want to be in sorting these out.

Broken beans: If the bean has not been otherwise compromised by mold or erosion, a broken bean, or an "ear" (a bean that has the middle part broken out from the outer part), is not an issue beyond its cosmetic appearance.

Quakers: Very light-colored beans that do not roast to a dark color are called quakers. These are typically unripe or under-developed beans. Usually, these are also only a cosmetic issue. If your coffee has a lot of quakers, you might want to pick a handful of them out and grind and brew them separately to find out how they taste. This will let you know if they will significantly impact the flavor of your coffee. It's hard to tell if a bean is a quaker before you roast it, so quakers are generally removed after roasting.

BEAN DEFECTS

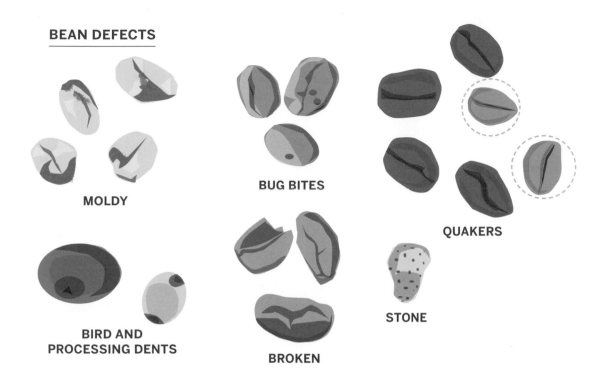

MOLDY

BUG BITES

QUAKERS

BIRD AND
PROCESSING DENTS

BROKEN

STONE

ARABICA BEANS

Chaff

Bug bites: The common coffee beetle likes to burrow through the beans in the ripe fruit. These beetles are everywhere, so it's normal to find a few beans in every batch with holes in them. Sometimes their tunnels can trap debris and cause green mold. While this mold is probably not harmful, it's best to remove any beans with holes.

Dents: Many species of birds peck at coffee cherries. The pointed tips of their beaks leave rounded marks on the beans. These marks usually have no impact on the quality of the bean. Beans dinged in processing also have a similar dent.

Moldy beans: Despite alarming claims you may have heard, significant mold is rare in coffee that is dried and stored properly (the typical standard is less than 12 percent moisture within the bean). Most tests show less mold on coffee beans than on tomatoes, strawberries, and other foods. Even so, it's best to remove any individual bean that may be moldy. That includes the bug-bitten beans previously mentioned, but also includes any broken bean that shows discoloration along the broken edge.

In rare cases, beans that were improperly stored in wet conditions might develop a very obvious surface mold that is powdery and has a whitish color. This is easily visible and has a strong, musty, unpleasant odor. You will not find individual beans with this issue. If it occurs, the entire lot will have the problem and should be discarded. Do not use moldy beans. *One special exception:* Similar to cheese, some beans are purposefully aged to develop a certain type of controlled molding, or fermenting. This is referred to as "monsooning" beans. In the days when beans were transported on sailing ships, beans traveled for months in the holds of ships on the high seas, so all beans were basically "monsooned" before arrival at port. Today, monsooning is a deliberate process, not an accident. If a bean was monsooned, it will say so in its advertising.

Chaffy beans: People are often concerned about chaff, fearing chaffy beans are moldy or unhealthy. But chaff, also called silverskin, is a normal part of the bean. You will see a lot of chaff on beans that are dry processed, and almost no chaff on wet-processed beans that were washed throughout their processing. Chaff is not a problem in terms of health or taste. It is, however, flammable. If you have a lot of chaff, it's good to shake the beans in a coarse sieve or colander to remove most of the chaff before roasting to avoid the possibility of the chaff catching fire during roasting.

Inspecting freshly roasted coffee beans for defects

BEAN DEFECTS

Roasted beans showing the defective beans separated from the good beans.

National USA Brand

World's Top-Selling Brand

Popular Donut Shop Brand

Hand-Sorted Beans

Coffee beans cooling
in a cooling cylinder
after roasting

Defective Beans in Commercial Production

I have rarely known a coffee shop or small roaster who fully checks their green beans before roasting. Often, they do a cursory inspection after roasting and remove obvious offenders. But the standard I encourage roasters to maintain is to *inspect the beans before roasting*.

The pictures on pages 76 and 77 are a rather disturbing example of why this can be important. These pictures show beans purchased at a supermarket and poured out on a table for inspection. Two are from top-volume American coffee companies. The third is from the world's largest-volume coffee retailer and wholesaler. The fourth shows beans that have been hand-sorted.

The first picture shows beans from a national USA brand, and it is their top-selling branded blend. Note that it contains over 20 percent defects, which means it does not even qualify as "Exchange Grade" on standard charts of coffee quality. The second picture is from the world's top-selling brand and is equally disturbing, as it also contains over 15 percent defects—and is from their most expensive line of espresso, whole-bean products. The third picture is from a popular national donut-shop retailer. Note the lack of defects. This is clean coffee with proper sorting technique. Hand sorting the beans, as seen in picture four, is the best way to ensure your beans are defect-free.

Specialty Coffee Association of America (SCA) Green Coffee Classification

The green coffee classification standard provided by the SCA offers a basic guide for labeling a specific green-bean lot with a name that helps buyers know how many defects they can expect to encounter and how "clean" the finished beans are.

To classify a coffee, 300 grams of properly hulled coffee is examined for defects. There are secondary documents that list specific faults that might exist in certain regions but not in others. The coffees are also roasted and cupped to evaluate cup characteristics.

Specialty Grade (1): No more than five full defects in 300 grams of coffee. No primary defects allowed. A maximum of 5 percent above or below screen size indicated is tolerated. Must possess at least one distinctive attribute in the body, flavor, aroma, or acidity. Must be free of faults and taints. No quakers are permitted. Moisture content is between 9 and 13 percent.

Premium Grade (2): No more than eight full defects in 300 grams. Primary defects are permitted. A maximum of 5 percent above or below screen size indicated is tolerated. Must possess at least one distinctive attribute in the body, flavor, aroma, or acidity. Must be free of faults and may contain only three quakers. Moisture content is between 9 and 13 percent.

Exchange Grade (3): Allows 9 to 23 full defects in 300 grams. Must have 50 percent by weight above screen size 15 with no more than 5 percent of screen size below 14. No cup faults are permitted, and a maximum of five quakers are allowed. Moisture content is between 9 and 13 percent.

Below Standard Grade (4): Allows 24 to 86 defects in 300 grams.

Off Grade (5): More than 86 defects in 300 grams.

"Full defects" include black beans, moldy beans, significant foreign objects, fruit or leaves/sticks. "Primary defects" include parchment/husks, broken/chipped beans, insect damage, floaters/quakers, small stones, tiny objects.

The grade given to a coffee lot after evaluation will affect the price it can expect to fetch on the market.

Now that you know what to look for, you might want to start looking hard at the coffee you buy in stores to see the real quality. Hopefully, you want to make sure that the coffee you roast and offer to others is clean and meets Specialty Grade standards. Your ability to control the quality of the coffee you drink is one of the great perks of being a coffee roaster!

Your Roasting Area

Before you start roasting beans, consider the whole process from start to finish. Where will you locate the roasting device for good ventilation? How will you cool the beans? How will you store the cooled beans?

Beans get hot enough to cause serious burns. They can even burst into flames if you neglect the roast. Never leave a roasting device while it is still roasting! You should have padded gloves or other heat protection to handle the beans or trays after roasting.

Some basic equipment you should have in your roasting area as you prepare for your roast:

Highly insulated gloves: Grill gloves, which are easy to find, work well.

Water: Keep enough on hand to douse any bean or chaff fires. Do not use water on equipment with enclosed electronics, like an air popper.

Weighing scale: Use one that covers a weight range greater than the maximum weight of beans you can roast at one time.

Scoop or funnel: Use whatever is best for pouring the beans into the roaster without spillage.

INSULATED GLOVES

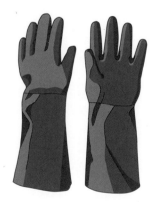

If you are going to be handling pans or drums with hot beans in them, temperatures can reach 500°F and you need double-insulated gloves and a great deal of care in cooling the beans

Bowls: Plan on using separate bowls for green beans and roasted beans.

Ventilation source: Ventilate smoke to the outside or use an adequate air filtration system.

Cooling device: Examples are a fan and cooling tray as well as stirring spoons, spatula, or squeegee to keep the beans moving while cooling.

Roast color chart: Printed material showing color ranges identified with roast names (Light, City, Dark, etc.) and/or temperature guidelines.

SCREEN SIFTER

This is a small bean screen gauge used to quickly assess the dimensions of a lot. If it is a Size 16 screen, that means beans of 16 mm widths will not pass through the holes.

Batch Size

Most roasters have a sweet spot for the weight and volumes they are optimally equipped to roast. You may find that a drum roaster rated for 8 pounds can actually roast 9 or 10 pounds with good results. However, at some point you will note that the cascading action of the beans has changed due to the extra weight and volume, and roast quality can deteriorate.

It's good to find your roaster's "sweet spot" for best results at different roast levels. Darker roasts take longer to develop. If you stretch your roasting curve too long for a dark roast, the taste profile will be flat and bland, so you will want to use smaller weights than with a light roast. You might find that you can roast 12 ounces of screen 16 beans for a medium roast . . . but only 8 or 10 ounces for a dark roast. (Screen size refers to the minimum measure of holes in millimeters that beans will not fall through when sifted on the screen. Sixteen-screen beans will not fall through a 16mm hole.)

You may want to roast each type of bean separately when making blends that require different bean types with different optimal roasting curves. Most roasting devices offer guidelines on minimum and maximum weights; follow those when determining how much of each bean you roast. (For example, if you want to make 16 pounds of coffee and use 12 pounds for your base bean and only 4 pounds for the other bean, you'll need to have a roaster that can handle a minimum of 4 pounds and a maximum of 12 pounds or more.) If your roaster does not offer guidelines, you'll need to experiment. I like to put my roasting batches in separate bags with good labels showing the bean name, temperature or roast designation (City, Dark, etc.), and weight in the bag. I line them up in the order I want to roast them and work my way through. I have large bowls on a table next to the roaster into which I put each component of a blend until I'm ready to stir them thoroughly and bag them.

Equipment Settings

For all of your roasting equipment, it is important to always read the manuals. Be aware of the options for controlling a roast and how to use those controls safely. Large roasters need a warm-up period; they also need to cool down to specific temperatures before they are shut off or metal parts may warp and cause issues over time. Make sure your machine is clean and has no chaff or oil buildup anywhere in the airflow, which could cause a fire.

On most commercial roasters, there is a safety shutoff device to prevent fires; it can be set to whatever temperature you want. Typically, this cutoff should be set to 500°F or below. The setting should be determined by the maximum safe roast level and the maximum temperature you expect to reach when you make changes, such as dumping the beans.

Airflow is usually expressed as numbers from 1 through 10; you might start roasting at 3, move the dial to 7 when the beans reach the development phase, and then set it to 10 to help the machine cool down between roasts. Keep in mind that you must lower the flame and heat level when you increase the airflow to avoid overheating the roaster.

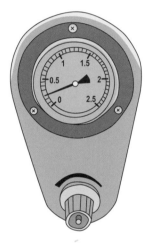

TEMPERATURE DIAL: An example of a heat gauge used on a gas-fired drum roaster. It does not measure temperature, it only shows the flame size or volume. You might adjust your roast to a higher or lower setting here in order to shorten the time overall, or in a temporary correction for a purpose such as optimizing a development period or initial warming up.

Most drum roasters use an ambient temperature somewhere between 430°F and 480°F after initial warm-up. The flame is adjusted to keep the ambient air between these ranges during roasting.

Roasting Times

The timing of a roast varies greatly, depending on the type of roaster used. Commercial fluid-bed roasters have very hot air temperatures and short roasting times. Drum roasters typically vary between 10 and 18 minutes, based on the roast level desired and the taste profile. A Costa Rican farmer I know swears by a 24-minute, slow "chocolate roast" for his Arabica Catuai beans. Most American roasters believe that a slow roast results in a "baked profile" due to a poor temperature-rise gradient, yet this farmer's coffee is delicious. He has dozens of clients in the United States to whom he ships his coffee after they have fallen in love with it at his shop in Costa Rica.

Generally, small home roasters take longer than large-volume roasters. The Behmor has an average roasting time of 18 to 20 minutes for 10 ounces, whereas its bigger brothers in the industry can drum-roast 20 pounds in 12 minutes.

If you are roasting for espresso beans or cold brew coffee, you will want to extend the roasting time by about 20 percent and reduce the heat to accommodate this. The slower time dries out the beans more, making them more porous for steam or hot-water forced extraction. More solids and flavor will be pushed into the brew. Slower roasting times also make sense for beans used in cold brewing. Coffee that is more porous will brew faster and have a sweeter profile.

Most bean types and varieties do not necessitate significant changes to basic formulas. Most Arabica beans are screened and selected to be fairly uniform in size, generally around 16-screen. However, there are some exceptions:

Peaberries: These are unsplit, round beans that are about 40 percent greater in mass and density than their sister beans. They need to be observed during roasting for different behaviors, such as lack of an audible first crack. You will likely need a specific roast program for them.

Tiny beans: Often peaberries, these specialty beans can be as small as eight-screen. They roast faster than heavier, larger beans, and should get a reduced flame.

Ungraded beans: These can be wild-grown beans sold by farmers who lack sorting equipment or a leftover lot after the farmer has presorted the other beans into specific sizes. They can also be a species like Excelsa that simply have a wide variance in size and shape. A simple rule of thumb is to roast beans like these to a finish temperature at least 5°F higher than graded beans to help bring the slower-roasting beans into an acceptable range. You may also need to remove some of the beans that simply didn't make the "color cut."

Humidity and starting temperature: Be aware that a difference in the starting temperature of the beans can change your timing. If you normally store beans in a room that is 68°F, but today you carried a new shipment of beans in your car during 10°F weather for three hours, you'll need to adjust your roast time to accommodate the lower temperature your cold beans will cause at the start. The same is true for beans left exposed to humid summer air; they may roast more slowly.

Expert tip: Never assume that any two different lots or seasons of the same beans will roast the same or have the same optimal roast level. For example, every time I get a new crop of Liberica, I do multiple tests to find our customers' favorite taste profile. The finish temperature can vary from 435°F to 455°F, depending on the beans and the season. Don't be afraid to recalibrate every season, even with familiar beans.

PEABERRIES

Peaberries are unsplit beans, so they often have greater mass than what we think of as a single bean (which is actually half of a split bean). This greater mass and density can create a sharper or nuttier flavor, and also render your standard S curves for non-peaberries inaccurate. Always start from scratch when trying to profile peaberries.

CHAPTER 5
THE ROAST PROGRESSION

The Science of the Roast

As coffee roasts, it changes color, aroma, and moisture content. It progresses through flavor conversions and acidity changes. The speed at which the changes take place and the final maximum temperature reached will change the taste profile, how porous the beans will be, and how many solids will dissolve into the brew. Being a successful roaster means having some understanding of what is taking place and trying to direct the roast toward the final product you desire.

An understanding of the changes that take place during roasting helps guide us toward obtaining specific results rather than just learning from trial and error and wondering why we got the results we did. Knowledge is power, and it also prevents us from wasting valuable time and coffee beans in trial-and-error learning.

The most basic changes, and how and when they occur, are discussed in this chapter.

OPPOSITE PAGE: Collage of coffee beans at different stages of roasting

SUGAR AND AMINO ACID CONVERSION

The Maillard reaction (pronounced my•*yar*) is a chemical reaction between amino acids and sugars during cooking that gives browned foods a distinctive flavor. We all recognize the smell of baking bread, and we recognize this aroma during coffee roasting. It is most prominent around temperatures between 350°F and 390°F, and it can sometimes be perceived as an aroma component up around the 420°F range. It progresses from a yeasty sort of baking aroma to one more reminiscent of toasted bread. It is named after the French chemist Louis Camille Maillard, who first described this reaction in 1912.

MOISTURE LOSS

As beans roast, they lose moisture. Typically, they will lose about 13 percent in a light roast and 17 percent or more in a darker roast. You need to account for this. If you roast three pounds of green beans, you will not get three pounds of roasted beans!

DENSITY AND POROSITY

As beans roast, the density decreases and porosity increases. They start as hard, dense stones and become more breakable and brittle as they roast. You can experience this easily by chewing on beans roasted at different levels. A light-roast bean is hard to chew and will not break down completely. A darker roast might crunch easily and reduce to a fine particle size in your mouth fairly rapidly. You'll notice that when people produce chocolate-covered espresso beans, they generally use a dark, slow roast to make the beans suitable to chew and swallow as a candy. Using a light roast for a chewable candy could be harmful to sensitive teeth, as the beans will be harder to break into small pieces. Using a slower, somewhat darker roast is generally good for espresso, since it increases the porosity and extraction of solids into the brew.

ACIDITY

A lightly roasted bean will be more acidic than a medium or dark roast. In this case, I am referring to a basic hydrogen ionic content; a liquid brewed from light-roast beans measures less acidic on the pH acid/base scale than a darker roast. Neutral is defined as a reading of 7.0. If a substance has more acid ions than neutral, it is called acidic. If it has less, it is called base or alkaline. Typical measurements of common foods are:

2.0   Vinegar

3.0   Grapefruit juice

4.0   Tomato juice

4.3 to 5.6   Coffee

6.0   Cow's milk, egg yolk

7.0   Neutral water

8.0   Sea water

9.0   Baking soda

The scale is logarithmic, meaning that each single digit is 10 times different from the one above or below it. A pH of 6.0 has 10 times fewer hydrogen ions per measured unit than a pH of 5.0. A pH of 4.0 has 10 times more than a pH of 5.0. Thus, going from 6.0 to 4.0 is a 100 times increase in acid ions.

When using the word "acid" in a discussion of coffee, we are not necessarily referring to pH. Many of the acids in coffee have a more alkaline pH than the brewed coffee. They are

called acids for reasons of chemical definition. Some of the acids that are formed or increased during roasting may affect the taste but not lower the pH.

Chlorogenic acids (CGAs) are more abundant in coffee than in any other plant-based food. They affect flavor and overall pH balance. But coffee also contains quinic, lactic, malic, citric, and acetic acids. Most of these acids are reduced by heat, but some acids begin to form when coffee is significantly over-roasted, and these often can have an irritating effect on our bodies.

Chlorogenic acid measurements are typically 6 or 7 percent in Arabica and up to 10 percent in Robusta. However, Robusta tends to produce lower pH readings when brewed. During roasting, chlorogenic acids slowly decompose to form caffeic and quinic acid. About 50 percent of the original CGAs are lost in a medium roast.

In general, coffee acidity is reduced by these factors:

- Lower-altitude growing

- Shade growing

- Natural sun drying

- Certain genetic varieties

- Longer, darker roasting

Acidity is a concern for many coffee drinkers. If coffee tends to bother their stomachs, they may be able to drink coffees that are at a pH of 5.1 or higher without discomfort. I regularly test commercial coffees purchased from the big chains and find that most of the time a medium roast has a pH level of 4.9 or under. Yet my own coffees typically test at 5.2 to 5.6. I attribute this to my slower roasting times (15 to 18 minutes versus a common industry practice of

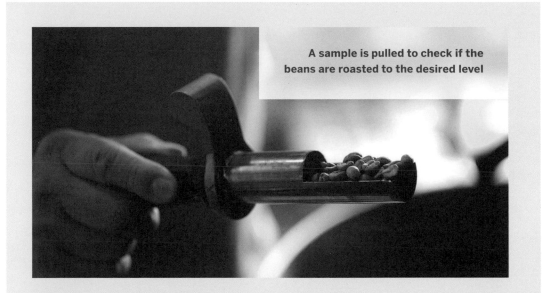

A sample is pulled to check if the beans are roasted to the desired level

SAMPLE ROASTING

Roasters do not want to waste large volumes of beans on experiments with temperatures and time. They generally have a very small roaster that is used for these Research and Development (R&D) experiments before going to the large roaster. Once a recipe is settled on, they will then try to scale it up for the larger roaster, hoping to get the same results and tweaking the recipe as needed.

If you are roasting on small home devices, every roast is what is normally considered a sample-size roast. If your roaster does not provide reproducible results, you have no control sample point or usable data from any one roast result. If you can't document what made your sample unique and transfer that data to a larger roaster, then you can't expect your scale-up to work. You're really still in the realm of trial and error.

If you are working with larger roasting machines, you want to use a sample roaster that provides reproducible results first, to run volumes of typically three ounces to eight ounces as tests. This is enough coffee with which to do cupping, aging, and other tests.

The simple guiding rule is to know what you are testing with each sample. For example, you might make a matrix of temperature versus time, or a matrix of the level of chocolate tones versus roast temperature and color. Try to reduce the number of sample roasts to the smallest amount that will yield the comparative results you want, and then cup and evaluate these tests, preferably after a period of resting. Use the results to guide your larger-volume roast recipe development.

12 minutes) and purchasing beans that are well sorted to eliminate unripe beans and defects. I recommend that all roasters keep an eye on their coffee's pH by purchasing a simple pH meter like the Milwaukee type, generally available for $30 or less:

ANTIOXIDANTS

Coffee contains high concentrations of antioxidants; these are only activated for use in our bodies after they are subjected to temperatures of at least 170°F. There might be 200 to 550mg of antioxidants per six-ounce cup in a medium

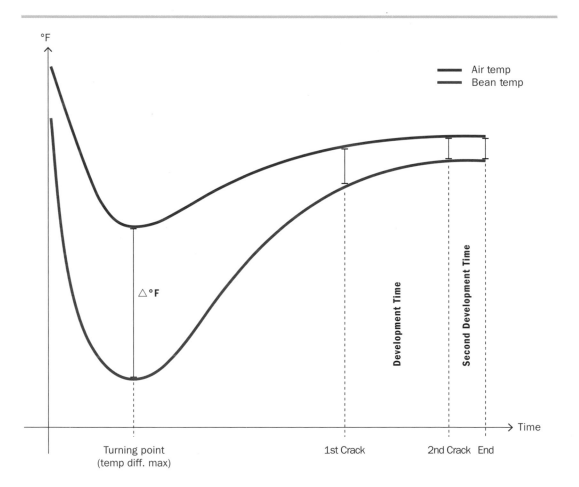

roast—a level far exceeding that of green tea and most other beverages considered high in antioxidants. As a roast progresses, antioxidants are destroyed, so lighter roasts contain the highest concentrations.

The Roasting (S) Curve

The Roasting (S) Curve is simply a graphical plot of time versus color or temperature level. It is called an S Curve because of its shape, but most roasters prefer to simply use the term "Roasting Curve." After you have your curve plotted you can populate it with notes.

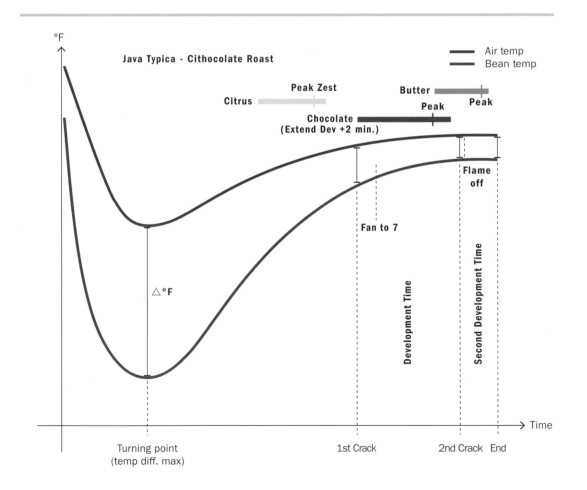

The roasting curve can be created manually by observation, or it can be produced by software that is responsive to sensors and data produced by the roasting device. If it is a software-generated curve, it might be used to control subsequent roasts. Generally, the curve is used to achieve certain results, so you will either pull samples or entire lots at certain times to compare and contrast later, often by a "cupping" procedure—a very specific type of brewing test to analyze the taste of the coffee.

An alternative to creating a literal roasting curve is to try different temperature settings and lengths of roasts, and pull samples along the way at specific markers, such as every 10°F. You can create a chart or log of the flavor notes at each point, and then contrast the results with different temperature and time experiments.

In the end, you are creating recipes for specific products, like a "Medium Roast Sumatra Lintong" or a "Chocolate Roast Villalobos." When you want to reproduce a predefined product, whether for your own consumption or for sale, you will follow the recipe you created for it.

Every Bean Is Unique!

Most consumers think of coffee as a simple concept, in which beans pretty much look alike and are only differentiated in taste by roast level. After all, they all look fairly similar when roasted (and definitely when ground!). This is why when we ask most of our customers what type of coffee they like, they most often answer first with a roast preference such as "I like Dark Roast." If pressed further they usually say something like "I like Sumatra."

In reality, coffee genetics are very diverse and it is the genetic variety and processing method (sun-dried, washed, etc.) that more often determine the taste they prefer.

Coffee cherries of
varying ripeness

SIMPLIFIED ROAST COLOR CHART

There are two basic types of charts available to identify standard colors of the roast for naming purposes. One is a collection of color squares bound together on a loose ring or in a binder, with fine gradations between them, and name or number labels. There might be dozens of sample color squares with minute differences between them, or you might use a simple chart like the one reproduced on page 97. This is a chart I developed for quick and simple identification of roast level. There are seven colors representing the most common terms and roast points. While many people use different and sometimes conflicting names for roast colors, I picked what we feel are recognizable and common names, ranging from what we have termed "Blond (Cinnamon)" to "French Roast."

I assigned temperatures to each, but these are just guides. Every machine will run a slightly different temperature for these colors. Periodically, I pull a few beans and put them on the chart, squinting my eyes to blur the details and try to see on which square the beans visually "disappear."

Be careful of hot beans—they can burn you and melt or scorch the chart. Handle them carefully and only place them on the chart briefly, or use a thin layer of glass on top of the chart. If you are not doing quick checks as you are roasting, let them cool before putting them on the chart.

This chart simplifies the many roast designations into seven useful steps for home roasters. The displayed temperatures are relative to one another and based on an industry-standard 10-pound roaster. Use them as a guideline only. Place a few roasted beans on the color swatches until you find the one that matches best.

1
BLOND
410°F

2
LIGHT
420°F

3
CITY
430°F

4
MEDIUM
440°F

5
FULL CITY
450°F

6
DARK
460°F

7
FRENCH
470°F

Tip: Light roasts preserve a wider range of bean flavors but lack the caramel-like tones of darker roasts. Light roasts are more acidic. Dark roasts are lower in acid, have more body, and bring out butter and caramel tones but lose the sweet, fruity profile of light roasts. Espressos should be roasted 10 to 20 percent slower to help dry out the beans and provide better extraction.

Stages of the Roast

As the beans roast, changes happen quickly. It's good to know what to expect ahead of time, because by the time you can pull samples and inspect them, the beans are moving through the next stage. Also, remember that there is a lag time after removing the beans from the heat source, during which they are still roasting from their own exothermic heat. You want to pull the beans just as they are entering the color stage you want, and you can expect a little further color development as they cool.

BROWNING

The beans go through several browning stages before they reach a level at which most consumers would brew them. The aromas given off may resemble hay, baking bread, and toast as the roast progresses from 320°F up to 375°F. This is typical of Arabica. You may find that Robusta and other species do not exhibit this same aroma progression.

FIRST CRACK

As the beans approach 390°F, they will exhibit a phenomenon called "first crack." This happens when the outer part of the bean dries and the moisture inside expands rapidly, converting to steam, thus cracking and expanding the bean. It is usually accompanied by a fairly loud cracking or popping sound.

CINNAMON/VERY LIGHT ROAST
Temperature range ~395°F to 410°F

The color of the beans as they enter first crack is usually referred to as Cinnamon. I like to call it "Blond" because novices assume that the term Cinnamon refers to taste.

CINNAMON/VERY LIGHT ROAST

LIGHT ROAST

Temperature range ~410°F to 425°F

As the beans finish first crack, which takes around 1 or 2 minutes, they are considered to be a Light Roast. Some roasters use the term New England Roast or American Roast for the lighter side of this level. The beans are removed from the heat at the peak of first crack. There will still be some cracking when you dump the beans into the cooling device. The toasty taste and aroma are present as well as brown sugar notes and a distinct lemon or citrus note. Citrus notes may progress from a sour lemon-juice taste and aroma to one that is less sour.

CITY ROAST

Temperature range ~425°F to 435°F

City Roast is usually defined as the color of beans taken out of the heating cycle about a minute after the tail end of first crack. By the time they are removed and cooled, almost all have cracked, and there is a light brown color to the roast. At this stage there are still all the original nuances of flavor and possibly some citrus tones; not much Maillard reaction or caramelization has occurred yet. Chocolate tones have also not developed, and acidity is still fairly high.

MEDIUM TO FULL CITY+ ROAST

Temperature range ~435°F to 445°F

Medium Roast is defined as having a significant amount of development time after the first crack has taken place. The minimum amount of time is 60 seconds or so past audible first cracking. The beans are smoothing out on the exterior, the color is deepening, and some caramelization is taking place, bringing out some of the butter, caramel, and chocolate tones. Fruitier, sweeter, citrusy, and the more floral notes start to diminish. You are in the Medium to Full City range until you begin to approach the second crack stage. As two minutes or more pass after first crack, the roast might be termed Full City+.

SECOND CRACK

The roast does not enter the next defined stage until second crack begins and is sustained for at least 30 seconds. When the core of the bean begins to reach the same temperature as the outer bean, the smaller pockets of water vapor within the core begin to steam, causing second crack to occur. The beans will further expand in size. While first crack is generally characterized by loud and distinct pops, second crack is often quiet, sounding like milk being poured on crisped rice cereal—a lot of small crackling sounds.

DARK ROAST (VIENNA)
Temperature range ~445°F to 455°F

Dark Roast is not a consistently used term. It applies to beans taken off heat in the late part of the ongoing second crack to beans taken from the heat within a few seconds after the end of second crack. Second crack can end gradually; somewhere between 2 or 3 minutes after the start of second crack, the beans pass into a darker color that is often referred to as Vienna Roast. As Dark Roast progresses, the beans begin losing their origin taste profile and start to take on a roast profile. What this means is that this level of roast and scorching creates similar tastes in all beans, so the individual identity of the bean gives way to a more common identity defined by the dark roasting itself.

FURTHER DEVELOPMENT

After the end of second crack, there is a brief period of 1 or 2 minutes of secondary development in which the beans are fairly quiet, but their color is darkening. The beans are starting to carbonize, and the roast profile gradually increases its dominance over the origin flavor profile.

FRENCH ROAST

Temperature range ~460°F to 465°F

French Roast occurs when the beans have fully gone through a second development period following second crack. As the roast goes past Vienna stage, the color typically starts to become a brown/black color. French Roast is NOT black—when you look closely at the dark beans you will see they are a very dark brown but not black. There is usually a significant amount of smoke generated at this stage, and this smoke and carbonization taking place in the beans are what give French Roast its toasty taste and aroma. If you aren't getting the toasty taste, you are not at French Roast yet. You are losing about 70 percent of the original profile taste now, in favor of the toasty, buttery smooth profile of a very dark roast. Chocolate tones may persist. All fruit and floral nuances are gone.

ITALIAN/SPANISH ROAST

Temperature range ~470°F to 480°F

Italian and Spanish Roast levels are generally something roasters stay away from. Almost all of the origin characteristics of the bean are lost, and the smoky flavor completely dominates. The beans are black and highly carbonized. This roast level is seldom intended for consumers who are brewing at home. It might be performed for a café looking for a distinct, super-dark roast flavor that is part of a signature offering. You are also flirting

with bean fires at this stage, which can flash up at any time due to a floating piece of chaff hitting a drop of oil on the outside of a bean. If you roast long enough, the beans might even ignite as they are being poured out, as they get a quick blast of oxygen from the outside air.

COOLING THE BEANS

There is a running debate about how much effect cooling times have on taste, but generally it is agreed that faster cooling is better. On some small machines, like the Behmor, you have no control over the cooling time (it is preset at 13 minutes), and on most larger machines, there is a cooling tray or device like a vortex cooler that will speed up the cooling process. It's important to drop the temperature below 200°F as quickly as possible so the beans are no longer roasting internally. My large drum roaster has a very effective cooling tray with a fan that draws air downward through the beans as they are stirred in a circle, and they're often cool to the touch within 3 to 4 minutes. This is optimal.

On my 20-pound grill roaster, I need to dump the beans onto a self-designed cooling tray with fans. This is something anybody can build; you make a simple frame about two feet wide and five feet long, mount radiator grill sheets or screens with perforated holes (preferably at least $1/16$-inch wide) inside the frame, then stand the fan(s) at one end and slide the cooled beans off the other end. Use scoops or stirrers to keep the beans in constant motion as the fan cools them. I can cool 20 pounds of beans in about 6 to 8 minutes, depending on roast level and the air temperature; this is an acceptable cooldown time.

CHAFF CONTROL

Chaff is very flammable. It can also get sticky if the beans are dark roast and oily. Most roaster fires are started because flaming chaff comes into contact with hot beans that have

A simple fact:
A proper roasting curve should result in beans that are the same color all the way through. If the outside of the bean is darker than the inside, the taste profile will probably be lacking. It might mean your time is too short or your temperature rise curve is not even. An easy way to check for uniform color throughout is to take a whole bean, a broken bean piece, a little coffee ground from the same bean lot, and place them on the color square you are trying to match. They should all correspond to that color.

Coffee chaff collected after the roasting of coffee beans

BASIC ROAST PROGRESSION QUICK REFERENCE

Roast Point	Browning	First Crack	Development Time	Second Crack	Second Development Time	Carbonizing
Temperature	310°F to 370°F	380°F to 395°F	400°F to 435°F	440°F to 450°F	455°F to 465°F	470°F+
Flavor Notes	Hay/ Bread/ Toast	Citrus/ Floral/ Baked Goods	Citrus/ Fruit/ Butter/ Brown Sugar	Caramel/ Butter/ Chocolate	Chocolate/ Extreme Butter/ Smoke	Charcoal

some oil on their surfaces, and the beans quickly ignite. Beans vary widely on how much chaff they cast off. My favorite Brazil Arabica beans that are naturally dried give off a massive amount of chaff, whereas the peaberry Robusta from Vietnam is thoroughly washed and gives off almost no chaff. I need to empty the chaff filter every three roasts for the Arabica but can go 12 roasts or more with the Robusta.

The way to control chaff is very different from one roasting device to another. It's important to make sure you are doing whatever you can to route the chaff into some sort of collection basket and ensure that it is not building up anywhere near the roasting beans. Check any chaff filters and the entire air pathway through which chaff travels to make sure nothing is clogging up and creating a fire hazard.

Chaff is wonderful stuff! It is full of nutrients, and you can easily find a gardener who will want to compost it or work it into their soil. I have a gardener who regularly picks up my bags of chaff for this purpose.

ROAST LEVELS

The following are examples of roasted beans that show the colors associated with the most common terms for those levels:

Cinnamon

Light

City/Medium

Full City

Dark

French

Italian

Roasting Quick Reference Guide

DRUM ROASTING QUICK REFERENCE

This quick reference guide shows the basic stages of roasting with a drum roaster, small or large. Temperature ranges are approximate and depend on your equipment, probes, and the bean type.

PRE-WARMING

If your roaster is small, such as a commercial sample roaster or a Behmor 1600, I recommend that you warm up the roaster a bit before the first roast of the day. This is especially important if you are pushing for 12 ounces or more at a dark roast. Start the roaster without the drum or chaff tray on a regular roast cycle and then shut it off completely after 30 to 45 seconds.

If you are using a larger drum roaster (three-pound capacity or more), it's important to run the machine at the lowest heat setting until the ambient temperature reaches 300°F. On my 10-pound roaster, I let the machine warm up for 30 minutes. Proper warm-up and cooldown of your roaster will help prevent warping of the machine drum and shaft.

POUR IN THE BEANS

In a small roaster, pour the beans into the drum, set it in place, and turn on the machine for the roast cycle or settings you want.

In a larger roaster, pour the beans into the hopper with the bottom slide closed. Then open the slide, start the timer, raise the heat to the setting you want to start the roast at, and set the air gauge to 3 (if your scale is 1 to 10) or equivalent. Close the bean hopper slide. The cool beans will reduce the ambient temperature in the roasting chamber, then "turn around" at approximately 160°F to 185°F and the ambient and bean temperatures will rise.

WATCH AND LISTEN FOR FIRST CRACK

Temperature range ~350°F to 390°F
Pull samples after 7 to 9 minutes if you can; if it's not possible, simply listen for the first loud popping, cracking sounds. Typically, beans go through browning phases before they crack. I call the basic stages "bread," "toast," and "citrus," as these

CONTINUED ON PAGE 108

DRUM ROASTER

The main components of drum roasters are generally very similar. Heat sources are applied to the drum, where the beans are tumbled 30 to 60 times per minute so they roast evenly. Electronic and mechanical controls allow this process to be adjusted and refined as the roast progresses.

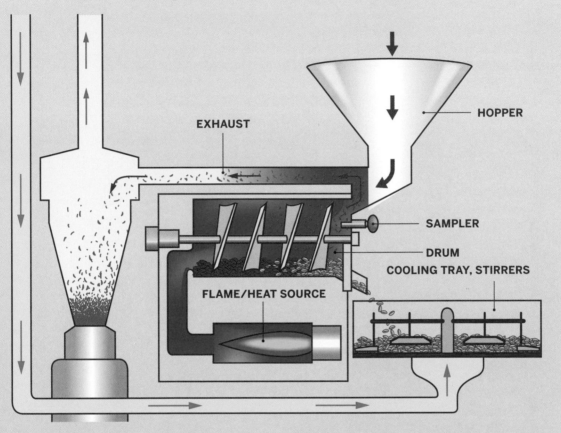

EXHAUST

HOPPER

SAMPLER

DRUM

COOLING TRAY, STIRRERS

FLAME/HEAT SOURCE

HOPPER: Here is where the beans are added to the drum. There is a slide at the bottom to stop or allow the flow of beans.

DRUM: The drum has angled blades to disperse the beans as they tumble.

SAMPLER: The sampler wand allows spot-checking at any time to check color and aroma.

FLAME/HEAT SOURCE: The heat is usually applied from the bottom, but some electric roasters have heat elements on the sides of the drum.

EXHAUST: The exhaust carries heated air and chaff through filters to the outside.

COOLING TRAY: A fan pulls air through the circulating beans to cool them quickly.

CONTINUED FROM PAGE 106

aromas develop in the browning process. Citrus may be pronounced or lacking, depending on the variety of beans.

FIRST CRACK

Temperature range ~380°F to 405°F

It may be hard to determine the start and end of first crack because beans never cooperate! It's like a bell curve, with the majority cracking in the middle. I call first crack "done" when only stragglers are popping. If you want a Cinnamon Roast or very light roast, you'll want to go into the cooling phase as the first crack is ending, or within a minute afterward. You will have an acidic, possibly citrusy, fruity taste profile, most likely with some butter, toast, and brown sugar elements.

ROAST CHARACTER DEVELOPMENT

Temperature range ~405°F to 445°F

In the 2 to 4 minutes after first crack has ended, the beans are moving into the caramelization stage, which burns off the brown sugar tones and starts development on the final, natural full-taste profile. Acidity will be reduced, and chocolate tones and some unique fruit notes might emerge and strengthen. The butter aroma and taste continue to increase. At this stage, many roasters will open the air valve to 7 or so and reduce the heat source to help vent smoke and lengthen the development stage. The beans are now becoming exothermic and providing a lot of the heat needed.

SECOND CRACK

Temperature range ~445°F to 465°F

The beans will start to crackle after the initial development period ends; they will pop and expand a little more. After 20 to 30 seconds, they will likely be in full

second crack. Second crack is tricky, so be careful! Some beans will go into second crack within 1 minute of the end of first crack, even if you lowered the ambient temperature. Others might take 4 or 5 minutes. Second crack can also go on for a long time, so if you find it lasting more than 3 minutes, you should make sure that you are not getting into too dark of a color range. If you pull at the start of second crack, you will have a Medium or Full City Roast. If you pull at the end, you will be entering Dark Roast. Within 2 to 4 minutes after second crack, you will be entering Vienna and then French Roast.

COOLDOWN

If you're using a small roaster, hit the cooldown button, or turn off the heat and turn on the fan. If you have the capability, dump the beans. Roasted beans are incredibly hot and will cause serious burns. Be very careful of the beans and all surfaces that have been heated in the process. Put the beans onto a long, wide cooling tray with a fan, and stir them as they cool.

If you're using a large roaster, turn on the cooling tray, pull the bean dumping lever, and turn the air dial to maximum, then lower the heat to its lowest setting. Cooling times are not that critical as long as you can get the beans below about 170°F within a few minutes. Ideally, beans should take between 3 and 8 minutes to become cool to the touch.

The Technological Future of Roasting

Coffee roasting in modern society presents challenges when it comes to obtaining proper permits and meeting environmental needs. Even backyard grill roasters might face issues with smoke traveling in unintended directions. Then there's the additional safety hazard of handling gas or propane fuel sources. We also need to look at the larger issue of the enormous amount of roasting done daily across the world, and what the impact might be to air quality.

Most of the solutions available today for reducing roasting emissions are expensive and bulky, and the manufacturers of emission control products do not generally work closely with the manufacturers of roasting equipment.

In the last three to four years quite a bit of R&D has been done to re-invent coffee roasting equipment as a stand-alone, integrated technology. New patents have been filed for machinery that takes a more comprehensive approach to heat sources, roasting, and emissions control, with the goal of creating "all-in-one" equipment solutions that address every aspect of roasting, safety, and environmental impact.

Bellwether Coffee in California created an integrated system that will roast about six pounds of beans and is entirely automated. It uses 240V AC electricity as a power source and has an emissions control built in that earned it an emissions-free certification. It can also connect to the Web and interface with a local tablet to store roaster profiles.

I have found this technology to be a huge step forward in creating easy, ecologically-sound solutions for people who need to produce a reasonable amount of volume for a coffee shop or small mail order operation. It's exciting to see advances like this that will eventually transform the nature of roasting in this volume range, which is a common level of volume needed for small roasting companies

Important Roasting Notes and Tips

Robusta, Liberica, Excelsa, and some Arabica origins are simply not consistent with the common scenario of first and second crack. This is why you watch and sample when dealing with a new origin, species, or variety, and why it is important to test and log your results. Robusta often has an almost silent first crack. It also might progress from second crack to burnt within two minutes. A professional roaster is not continually surprised by a bean that behaves atypically; they expect its behavior after watching how it performs the first few times.

The progression of all flavor notes through roasting temperature and times is not uniform. This is why it is helpful to establish your roasting curve for a specific bean and test it. For example, a Kenyan bean might have citrus notes to a fault and, if roasted poorly, become unpalatable when used in espresso. It might have a pH of 4.3 and taste like lemon juice. So the methodical roaster watches and tests that origin through the various stages and colors until it becomes apparent where the citrus begins to drop out and other characteristics come forward. This will likely create a much more palatable and pleasing coffee. Citrus may also be reduced by a slower roast with a lower rise of temperature in the 410°F to 430°F range.

Faults that appear in a flavor profile, such as overwhelming and objectionable notes like sour lemon, a musty taste, licorice, or a metallic taste, can often be the fault of the bean and how it was processed. Do not assume you are roasting poorly. Try other origins and see if the same roasting process gets the same negative results. If not, don't be afraid to blame the bean and purchase something different next time.

THIS PAGE: Top: Freshly roasted coffee beans. Bottom: Roaster pulls a sample of coffee beans during the roasting process

OPPOSITE PAGE: Coffee beans being poured into a commercial roasting machine

Neatly arranged coffee beans and cups of ground coffee for a tasting

PART III: AFTER THE ROAST

A man inhales the
aroma of coffee during
a tasting session

CHAPTER 6
CUPPING, TASTING, AND EVALUATING YOUR ROAST

What Is Cupping?

As we know from the different physiologies and preferences of consumers, it is hard to speak objectively about what makes coffee good or bad. How do you compare one cup of coffee to another? International organizations that hold competitions found it necessary to establish a common set of standards and protocols in order to have some basis on which to score the quality of beans and brews. There are different standards for espresso, for instance, than for drip coffee. Also, how does a buyer assess the quality of beans from different farms and regions? How can buyers have a reasonable guarantee that a coffee will be well received by consumers? How do we decide what the dollar value per pound of a coffee origin might be?

Eventually, a number of qualities were deemed important in how we perceive and enjoy coffee, and methods were established to evaluate coffees for purchasing and competitive events. One of these protocols is called "cupping," in which a set of procedures is performed consistently in order to compare the values and characteristics of different coffees. The most important initial step in cupping is to be sure that your sample size is large enough to truly represent a sampling or lot.

Cuppers roast and brew coffee according to a common roast and resting procedure, and brew many sample cups in order to be sure their sampling is substantial enough that it doesn't miss something. They compare these many cups and look for variance in them, then evaluate their tasting experience by filling out a scoring card to arrive at a composite number that should reflect the relative merit of that coffee lot.

Specialty Coffee Association (SCA) Standards for Cupping

Every roaster needs to be aware of the world standards of cupping in order to understand oft-quoted cupping scores and comments. In the United States, the standard normally used is set by the Specialty Coffee Association (SCA), and the guide is available in PDF form on their website (see Resources section on page 151).

Specialty Coffee Association of America Coffee Cupping Form

[NOTE: The SCA used to be called the SCAA (Specialty Coffee Association of America). When looking for reference from this source, don't be confused if it appears as SCAA or SCA.]

The purpose of SCA guidelines is not to mandate what is best for every coffee but to establish a set of rules by which coffees are consistently analyzed and compared. While it's a starting point, it may not actually serve your needs if you're not roasting Arabica or not using their chosen evaluation roast level, which corresponds roughly to City Roast.

Beyond establishing guidelines for competitive analysis, the cupping standards establish a baseline for how coffee is evaluated, rating each coffee using 10 different criteria. There is also a category for defects, which is a classification that deducts points. While a perfect score is 100, in reality nothing close to this value is reached.

The majority of Specialty Grade Coffees receive scores in the 82 to 90 range, with anything higher probably qualifying for a medal. The 10 rating criteria are **fragrance, aroma, flavor, aftertaste, acidity, body, balance, sweetness, uniformity,** and **cleanliness**. These terms have very specific definitions in cupping, so it is important to read the guide and understand what they mean.

**Coffee lined up and
ready for tasting**

The How and Why of Cupping

We cup to evaluate quality and have some means of comparison between coffees. The most important takeaway from professional cupping standards is an understanding of how you can rate coffees in a meaningful way and decide how "good" they are. Important procedures to keep in mind as you cup are:

1. **Use a consistent process:** Use the same equipment, initial brewing temperature, grind size, coffee weight per volume of water, device used to brew the coffee, and cup sample size.

2. **Sniff the coffee:** Immediately after grinding, hold the coffee within two inches of your nose and inhale two or three times. How does it compare with other coffees in terms of being compelling, rich, and flavorful? Do you smell butter, chocolate, fruit, or spice? Take notes.

3. **Evaluate the coffee as it cools:** To taste the evolution of the flavor profile as it cools, perform aroma and sipping tests at the start and then at five-minute intervals. Some origins are famous for providing startlingly different profiles between the first taste and the taste after the coffee has cooled for 15 minutes. This is important to know. Also, defects appear most prominently as the coffee sits. After cooling, the coffee should taste sweet and delicious. It may have developed caramel, butter, vanilla, or chocolate notes. If the cooled coffee is unpleasant, it is likely there were defective or unripe beans that are denaturing its taste through enzyme activity, or because they are leeching out of the solids dissolved in the brew.

4. **Use measuring equipment:** At minimum, you should have a scale, thermometer, and color chart

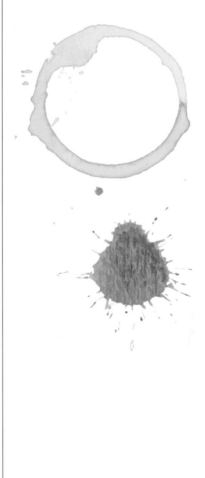

to determine weight, water temperature, and roast level. You may want to invest in a densitometer and pH meter.

5. **Develop your vocabulary:** Study the materials available online, including the SCA flavor-note chart (a link is provided in the Resources section, page 151). A good way to learn to identify aromas and flavor notes is to purchase some commercially roasted coffees that list flavor notes and see if you can identify them while brewing and drinking the coffee. Experience builds discernment.

6. **Establish your own cupping ritual:** If you are roasting on a Whirley Pop or popcorn air popper, there's only so much value you can derive from a cupping procedure, as your control over roast consistency is very limited. But if you have a device that can achieve predictable and consistent results, you might adopt a simple but useful evaluation process like the sample cupping procedure that follows.

SAMPLE CUPPING PROCEDURE

1. Use a scale to weigh out about 1 ounce of coffee (28 grams) in a 12-ounce French press. Use a Zojirushi (or other device like an office watercooler heater) so water temperature can always be tested at 195°F, or whatever the machine is set at (or use a thermometer).

2. Pour the coffee into the press, then the water. Wait 30 seconds, and stir the grinds thoroughly. Wait another three minutes, stir again, and press the plunger, then pour the coffee into small cups that always hold the same amount.

3. Sniff the aroma of the coffee in the cup before drinking it, then sip the coffee and write down your impressions of the attributes that are important to you. Sip again at five-minute intervals until it has cooled, and write those notes down as well. Keep a log for comparison purposes.

Evaluating Your Roast

Using some standard criteria to evaluate your roast helps you qualify your results and assist in describing and promoting your product to others. Here are the basic criteria used by most roasters:

ACIDITY

Some origins (like Kenya) are expected to be acidic, and some (like Sumatra) are not. You might compare acidity between coffees with similar acidity expectations if you are evaluating which Kenyan variety you prefer. Or you might compare coffees with different acidity expectations to evaluate whether you want to work with a Kenyan or a Sumatran coffee, based on whether you like high or low acidity. As previously discussed, acidity refers to pH and can be measured on a pH meter or test strip, but it also refers to sharpness or "attack," which is the first perception of the coffee on the front palate area and the aroma.

BODY/MOUTHFEEL

This generally refers to the viscosity or denseness of the coffee liquid and the amount of colloids and sucrose you can detect. High body is generally perceived more favorably than low body, although taste perceptions of body can be misleading when compared to actual measurements of dissolved solids and sugars.

AROMA

As previously discussed, aroma is of variable importance. People who love the aroma of coffee and can perceive its components best are typically people with more sensitive front-palate sensations, or, as the University of Florida labels them, "supertasters."

Aroma is not just perceived by the nose; it is sensed by the front part of the roof of the mouth. The qualities of aroma that most people respond to are the sweet/sourness of the aroma and the baked or caramel tones. "Aroma people" commonly say, "The smell wakes me up and energizes me" and "I don't care so much about how the coffee tastes; I really need the aroma." It makes sense to rate aroma if you're trying to give away or sell roasted coffee to people who really appreciate that aspect of coffee.

BALANCE

Complexity is generally affected by the amount of sugars and amino acids contained within the beans as well as minerals from rich soil and other components. Complex coffees are apt to have more depth and better balance. No single attribute dominates, and the overall sensation is pleasant. For example, if you have an acidic coffee that tastes like lemon juice when you use it as espresso, you have a coffee with very poor balance.

FLAVOR AND SWEETNESS

Is the coffee delicious? Does it have interesting flavor notes? Do you find yourself wanting another cup? Is it palatable without added cream and sugar? A good coffee should leave a good memory and a desire to have another cup; only a poor coffee needs cream and sugar to make it palatable. Adding cream and/or sugar to kick up interesting flavor notes is

OPPOSITE PAGE: A barista pours hot water into tasting cups, ensuring each is evenly filled so coffees are sampled under identical conditions.

simply a matter of interest or preference; it should not be necessary in order to make the coffee drinkable.

AFTERTASTE OR PERSISTENCE

I like to use the term "persistence" because the word "after-taste" seems to have a negative connotation in the United States. This term refers to the persistence of the taste profile and memory after you have swallowed it. Front-palate coffees, such as the Arabica Typica variety, have almost no persistence of memory, and people have a hard time picking out the coffee they just drank by matching it to other cups in a blind taste test. Robusta gives high back-palate stimulation and creates a strong memory. People typically have no trouble identifying it again in a blind taste test. That is why Robusta is often used in espressos—coffee purveyors want patrons to recall that great taste 20 minutes later and come back for another shot. Evaluating aftertaste can also guide you toward choices of coffees to include in blends, as you may want to balance different origins that have great acidity and initial attack but also leave a satisfying, lingering impression.

Testing Coffee Black Versus with Creamer and Sugar

The notion that coffee should be enjoyed black (without anything added) is commonly promoted in America and Europe but is not actually shared around the world. Advocates of drinking coffee black claim that it is the only way to perceive the entire taste profile of the coffee, unmasked by the buffering effect of creamer (cream, half-and-half, or milk) and/or sugar. Yet research does not support this finding, and whenever I travel in Central and South America or in the Caribbean, farmers tell me the exact opposite—that the acidity of coffee dulls the palate to the perception of many of the best flavor elements, and one can perceive the nuances of the coffee best if the acidity is buffered with milk and sugar.

In Central America, I commonly see farmers preparing their own coffee in the morning by heating a pitcher of milk on the stovetop and serving coffee by first pouring the hot milk into about a third of the cup they are using, then adding brewed coffee and usually two heaping tablespoons of raw sugar. I once commented to a farmer in Costa Rica that this reminded me of "coffee regular" in New England, which means coffee with two shots of cream or milk, and double sugar. He laughed and reminded me that Costa Rica used to supply quite a bit of the coffee to the popular donut-shop brands in New England and probably influenced our notions of how to drink it. He also cited research that indicated that more flavor elements are enhanced by creamer and sugar than are masked by it.

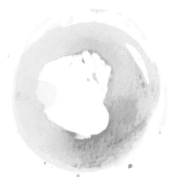

In Asia, few people drink coffee black. All the popular brands of instant coffees, such as San Miguel, Trung Nguyen G7, Vinacafé, Nescafé, and others, contain quite a bit of creamer and sugar. While some of the brands offer a black version, it sells so poorly that Highlands Coffee removed the black version of their popular Ready-To-Drink (RTD) canned Vietnamese Iced Coffee from the market in 2016 because it wasn't selling.

In my own research and experience, I have found that the flavor profiles of Arabicas, which are mostly front-palate coffees, are often masked to some degree by creamer and sugar, but certain tones are enhanced, particularly chocolate and butter tones. When I am cupping coffee with less than a three-day rest period, I first taste the coffee black, then add creamer, then sugar. Trying the coffee these successive ways helps me see exactly what is happening and helps buffer the woodiness and raw taste that might dominate in unrested coffee. I also believe that everybody has their own palate preferences and they need to use trial and error to see what works best for them. My own palate is overwhelmed by acidity, and I

A coffee grader skims the coffee grounds from the cup to test and inspect the quality of the roast.

find I can't taste the full profile of coffee that contains Arabica unless I buffer it a little with creamer. Your experience might be different. Trust your own perceptions!

Creamer and sugar have less of a muting effect on back-palate coffees, which makes sense, because we do not perceive sugar or fats as well in the back of the palate as we do in the front. In countries like Vietnam, where the majority of the coffee contains at least some Robusta, coffee is almost ubiquitously served with creamer and sugar (often in the form of sweetened condensed milk, which contains both whole milk and sugar).

The Importance of Resting

As we have discussed earlier, the chemical changes that take place in coffee during roasting are enormously complex and not fully documented or understood. As mandated in the SCA cupping guide, coffees should not be cupped immediately after the roast but after a variable period between 4 and 24 hours after roasting. This doesn't mean all coffees are done "resting" after 24 hours; it just provides an understanding that coffee should generally rest before evaluation or drinking.

It's critical to your understanding of evaluating your roasted coffee that you realize that chemical changes continue to occur in the coffee for weeks and even months *after* roasting. The most significant changes occur in the first few days, then the coffee settles into a slower process of aging over the course of months. Once coffee begins to become significantly stale, we lose interest in further changes. Here are a few guidelines for freshness based on handling:

"FRESH OFF THE ROAST"

A popular myth passed around in print is that there is something unique and irreproducible about the taste of coffee right off the roast. I often read statements like "There is nothing that can compare or measure up to the taste profile of coffee consumed immediately after roasting," and I know that the author of these words has never really done much comparison testing of coffees at different times within the first three days of roasting. In reality, almost every coffee will peak in flavor at some point after roasting within three days but almost never right off the roast. Immediately after the roast, the coffee is still undergoing changes related to combustion and generally has a woody, raw taste that is lacking in many of the mature tones that might develop later on.

While some coffees have a very pleasurable taste profile right off the roast, most don't. I have a series of coffees from the Poços de Caldas volcanic soil of Brazil that is delightful right off the roast. I also have a Sumatra Lintong that is unpalatable right off the roast. Both will proceed to develop their peak flavor within a few days. I can cup the Brazilian coffees immediately, but I simply won't cup the Lintong until the third day. It is woody and unidimensional, and it leaves an unpleasant aftertaste in early cupping. If I were forced to evaluate it prior to the third day, I couldn't give it a review that would place it in the Specialty Coffee category. But the transformation that takes place on the third and fourth days is astounding—it simply becomes a whole different coffee and gets a high cupping score.

THE THIRD DAY

I use the "Third Day" as a euphemism for the point at which the original woodiness and after-processes of combustion have disappeared and the coffee has developed its signature profile. Most coffee shops that roast their own coffee stop resting the freshly roasted coffee and start serving it to patrons after three days (72 hours). Coffee roasted on Monday may be served starting on Thursday. My neighborhood coffee shop serves their fresh roasted coffees between Day 3 and Day 7. They roast on a schedule so that a new roast reaches Day 3 as the previous roast passes Day 7.

A coffee shop usually features a few consistent offerings along with a "Coffee of the Day (or Week)." These are coffees that may persist on the menu for a few days or weeks that are dependent on availability from their providers. In such an ever-changing environment, shops tend to adopt a set policy on the number of days to rest and serve coffee and assume it covers most of their offerings. A more specialized roasting house may rely more on the retail of roasted, bagged beans rather than brewed cups of coffee. Because they may do more R&D, they will tend to have different rest times for different coffees, as appropriate.

THE EIGHTEENTH DAY

I use Day 18 as a catchall phrase for the time at which the coffee has peaked. Depending on how it has been packaged or stored, the coffee may stay at peak for some time or begin to slowly lose its wonderful, freshly roasted flavor. One of our bean sources in the Philippines has a commercial line called 18 Days, and they chose that name because of the generally accepted fact that coffee should not be sold as fresh roast coffee beyond 18 days. This can be a very misleading generalization, though, because the packaging and storage conditions may cause coffee to lose its flavor earlier than this time, or it might protect the flavor up to 15 months.

If we assume that beans are all being stored at room temperature in a dry place, then the variability in freshness is due to the quality of the barrier material and whether containers were purged of oxygen when packaged. If a small roaster simply pours beans into paper bags and seals the top, as often happens in the marketplaces of many countries, then the prime shelf life is only a few days. On the other end of the spectrum is the commercial roaster who vacuums the air out, then flushes the container with nitrogen and seals it. The ideal container is impermeable to air: either a bottle, can, or a bag made from a four-layer foil and plastic film.

Peet's® Coffee released an advertising campaign a few years ago that announced how proud they were to have the shortest span of time between roasting and the average time a consumer will take the bag off the supermarket shelf. That time was 90 days. Yes, it's true that commercial coffees spend weeks making the journey from the initial distribution site to manufacturing centers to smaller distribution centers to the

SAMPLE LOG

NAME	SPECIES	CROP	DATE	ROAST LEVEL	ROAST TYPE	TIME	NOTES
Brazil Adrano	Arabica Mix	2020	07/20/20	French/ 468°F	Espresso/ Dry	15 minutes	Smokes heavily; increase air to 7 at 400°F
Papua New Guinea wild grown	Arabica Mix	2020	07/21/20	City/ 435°F	Standard	12 minutes	Reduce heat to 30°F differential after first crack

BLANK SAMPLE LOG

NAME	SPECIES	CROP	DATE	ROAST LEVEL	ROAST TYPE	TIME	NOTES

retail stores that feature them. It is generally about 100 to 120 days before a consumer will take a bag home. Yet that bag of coffee still gives off a nice aroma and brews up tasting fresh at home, because it has been given the full vacuum/nitrogen-flush/four-ply barrier bag treatment.

Your own vacuum-sealed bags, if you choose this method, will probably give you two or three months of peak freshness. Without vacuum-sealing, expect only two or three weeks.

LOGGING YOUR ROASTS

It's important to keep logs so that your past experience can guide you. Depending on whether you are just pan roasting for fun or learning to use a commercial drum roaster, you want to record both the Roasting Curve (with notes marked on the chart) and your cupping comments and scores. Page 132 features an example of a simple log noting the coffee identity, roast levels, and cupping notes.

You probably will find over time what you prefer to record. A blank log form is provided to get you started. I also recommend that roasters post a white board or notepad on their roaster or in the immediate area to be used for simple comments like "Take the Brazil Dark profile down 2 degrees over the 7 to 10 minute mark to see if we get little better chocolate expression," or a similar note to help guide ongoing profile and roasting curve refinement. This practice not only reminds you later of ideas you have during roasting but also is a way to pass information between different people roasting on the machine. Your roasting software or controls might have no function available for making these sorts of notes and you might later remember there was an issue with something but not remember what it was!

Hot water being poured over the ground coffee beans atop a drip coffee maker

CHAPTER 7
STORING AND BREWING ROASTED COFFEE

About Storage

Proper coffee storage methods are debated widely, but an understanding of what proper storage is supposed to accomplish will guide you toward choosing your own best methods. There are some simple practices that can be adopted without buying anything new for storage, or you can invest a little money in a vacuum sealer or containers that allow air to be pumped out. After working so hard to create wonderful fresh roasted coffee, it's good to have a thorough understanding about how to keep it fresh and delicious for the longest possible time.

STORAGE METHODS

Coffee is deteriorated by oxygen, humidity, and drastic changes to its environment. Coffee is best stored in many small bags or containers rather than a large bin, and these should be opened as few times as possible. As much ambient air as possible should be squeezed or vacuumed out of the containers.

An unsealed bag of roasted coffee beans

VACUUM SEALING

This removes all the air from bags, but it can suck out some of the gases inside the beans that they need to remain stable. It is important not to overdo it when vacuum sealing.

HEAT SEALING

A completely airtight heat seal is important when storing in plastic or foil composite film bags; sealing it twice helps. For home use, I recommend a simple FoodSaver®-type machine and plastic freezer bags that are heat sealable. This type of machine both vacuums and seals.

NITROGEN FLUSHING

Nitrogen is inert and keeps oxygen away from the beans, preventing deterioration. The best way to store coffee is to first vacuum, then nitrogen flush, and finally heat-seal coffee. In comparison taste tests with coffee stored this way, consumers could not consistently distinguish between coffee that was a few weeks old or 12 to 15 months old.

REFRIGERATORS AND FREEZERS

Do NOT store coffee in a refrigerator or freezer. Subjecting coffee to drastic temperature alterations deteriorates the integrity of the beans, may result in frost crystals, and makes the bag film brittle and porous, letting unwanted refrigerator and freezer smells flavor your coffee. You cannot substantially affect the aging of coffee unless you can store it at -10°F, which is colder than any home freezer.

OPENED BAGS

I find the best way to keep a bag of beans fresh over a long time is to pour out enough for a few days' usage. Fold the top of the bag two or three times and wrap it tightly with a rubber band or tape. Leave it in a room-temperature location that is out of direct sun. Repeat after you use up the first amount you poured. Put simply, the fewer times you allow oxygen into that original bag, the longer it will keep.

STORAGE VESSELS

I find that most of my customers who have storage canisters at home think that pouring coffee from the bag in which they bought it into an open canister and putting the lid on is going to help keep the coffee fresher than keeping it in the original bag. This violates the most important principle of coffee storage—keeping air away from it. Every time the canister is opened, new air flows in. Here are some tips about how to choose the best types of containers to use and how to use the ones you may have to better effect.

PLASTIC BAGS

Never use food storage bags, such as sandwich bags. They are made out of film that is air permeable, and coffee will go stale quickly. Instead, use freezer bags. They are made of heavier material and have much less permeability to air and moisture. Squeeze the excess air out before sealing the top. I use freezer bags for quick storage of a few ounces of leftover beans or beans from small tests when I know I will be brewing or checking them within two or three days. The bags are convenient for this and will keep coffee fresh a few days. But no ordinary plastic food bag will keep coffee fresh for long.

MULTI-PLY PLASTIC OR FOIL BAGS

These have very low permeability and are designed to be almost as good as glass, plastic, or metal in terms of barrier effectiveness. They are flexible and can be folded over on top and resealed tightly with tape, a rubber band, or a tin tie, reducing the coffee's exposure to oxygen. This method is effective for large and small quantities.

GLASS OR OTHER IMPERMEABLE CANISTERS OR BINS

These are poor storage methods by themselves because every time they're opened, fresh oxygen is let in and sealed with the beans when the container is closed. However, they are great as a second-level container. Putting properly sealed bags inside a canister provides a double shield.

Note: Coffee retailers sometimes store beans in something like a mason jar immediately after roasting. Research has shown this creates internal pressure, which is an excellent stabilizer for coffee. This is for whole beans only and not for consuming the contents on an ongoing basis. Usually the pressure of the outgassing will eventually be too much for the

STORAGE METHODS

Vented Top Glass Containers

Air Pump Lid Plastic Containers

lid, so I turn the lid a little after the first few hours to release the pressure, then reseal it tightly. Done right, there will be a lot of pressure inside without deforming the lid. Many weeks later, when you release the lid with a POP, you'll be rewarded with the fresh-roast smell and excellent coffee quality.

MOVABLE LID CANISTERS

These are canisters with a lid that slides down onto the remaining coffee, usually expelling air through one-way valves as you push the lid down. While these containers are the best storage for an opened quantity of beans or grinds, they are usually quite expensive.

PUMP-VACUUM CANISTERS

These are canisters with a lid that can be pressed or pumped to expel a certain amount of air from inside the container, creating something of a vacuum within. These canisters are great at the start, but when the amount of stored coffee gets low inside the container, the amount of air vacuumed out becomes insignificant. The less coffee in the canister, the quicker it deteriorates.

Final Words on Freshness

Fresh is fresh: It doesn't matter what the calendar says or how the coffee is stored. Stale coffee is easily detected by aroma. To recognize the unmistakable smell that comes from stale coffee, you should deliberately sniff some really old coffees and compare the scent with fresh coffee. Thereafter, you can rely on your nose to decide whether coffee is still fresh enough to be enjoyable. There is some coffee that may smell a little stale but brew up nicely, although it won't be a perfect cup. Really stale coffee is awful.

Relying on taste and smell rather than calendar days can allow you to discover some interesting things. When I did some of my original Dalat Bourbon Arabica test roasts, I was frustrated by a back-palate bitterness that I couldn't seem to eliminate. This was early in my career and I hadn't yet fully come to appreciate the importance of resting coffee—I was cupping it within a few hours of roasting. A disappointing four-pound bag of medium roast got taped up and placed on a shelf and was completely forgotten about. Two months later I saw it again and decided to see if it was worth drinking or giving away. It smelled wonderful. When I brewed it, I was amazed that there was no bitterness and it was an excellent cup, full of buttery, chocolatey tones.

I figured my taste buds might be playing tricks on me, so I brewed and served it to one of my business partners and a couple of employees without any explanation. They exclaimed how good it was! For the next few days we enjoyed the rest of that bag and were continuously surprised by it. A couple of years later I saw a post on an SCA forum from a roaster who "confessed" that he felt Bourbon Arabica had a very long rest and maturation period; he liked it up to six weeks after the roast. Another roaster and I were quick to contribute our similar experiences to the thread.

Despite the performance of this "Methuselah" Bourbon, I have had the opposite experience with some coffees that simply went stale within three or four weeks, even with vacuum packaging. I have learned that there are no hard-and-fast rules about freshness or at what time coffees might be palatable after roasting. Trial and error are required.

Chemex

Brewing Coffee

Over the last 600 years or more, different peoples from around the world have created hundreds of ways to brew coffee. This book is not a place to describe all those methods in detail but rather to explain the basic differences and why different profiles are obtained from any methods that vary greatly in process.

Melitta type

DRIP METHODS

Historically, records indicate that coffee tended to be boiled in water in kettles before any drip methods were devised, then many dry-style methods were devised independently in different cultures. Electrical drip machines were developed first in the United States and Europe. The most important factors in drip-brew methodology are whether the brewing water is contacting all of the grinds equally, and whether the brewing finishes quickly enough to keep the coffee hot.

POUR-OVERS

Pour-overs are popular around the world, in variations such as the "sock brewer" in Central America (a mesh strainer positioned over a container vessel), the single-serve cup pour-overs (such as the Chemex), and other similar processes. These are pretty basic and make it difficult to achieve optimal results. In this process, gravity powers a drip of hot water through coffee grinds. Its faults include uneven distribution of hot water across the grounds, rapid cooling, and long wait time. If you are willing to pour the water near the top and then stir the grinds and water, you can improve saturation. You can also double-pour—take the brewed coffee and pour it back through the grinds. This will improve the quality but will also cool down the brew.

Phin filter

DRIP DEVICES

Drip devices perform a similar function to a pour-over but give you better control over temperature and saturation. In the United States, the ubiquitous Mr. Coffee is a common example. The issue with this style of brewer is that they normally have one to five jets of hot water pouring into the grinds. If you look at the grinds afterward, you will see that there are hills and valleys, showing that the jets over-brewed some grinds while under-brewing others. If using this type of machine, note that the style that has a hot plate under a glass carafe will provide uneven heat to the coffee as it sits after the brew and will scorch the brew slowly. It is better to go with the type that brews into an insulated stainless-steel carafe. The coffee will stay hot for maybe 45 minutes and will maintain a better taste.

The Vietnamese Phin filter is an example of a drip device. It spreads the water evenly over 100 or more tiny holes, dripping water through a thin substrate of coffee grounds. This method provides superior results when done properly. Be sure to use the right amount of coffee to deliver about a four-minute brew time; use very hot water, and preheat the receiving cup to help the brewed coffee retain its heat. The Phin is also used for making iced coffee. The best method is to use a tall glass, pour in any sweetener and creamer first, then pack the glass with cracked ice and place the brewer on top of the glass. The brewing is very picturesque, and the slow drip over the cracked ice produces less melt than if the brewed coffee were to come in contact with all the ice at once.

All drip devices still rely on gravity and are not "full immersion" methods. Some do a better job than others of distributing the water evenly across the grinds.

PERCOLATORS AND URNS

Percolators and urns were ubiquitous in American households and diners in the 1950s and 1960s. They actually brew well, due to an interesting fact of molecular chemistry: The flavor molecules in coffee have a certain viscosity that allows them to only reach a certain level in the brewing water. When the concentration gets thick enough, the brewed coffee acts as a barrier to further extraction. A percolator circulates coffee that has already passed through the grounds, from the bottom of the chamber to a fountain at the top (usually inside a glass top that allows you to see the coffee color). As it gets to the right density, it has a self-limiting effect on over-brewing. Percolators fell out of favor because they have a long brew time, usually two to four times as long as a drip brewer. But recently there has been a resurgence of this style of brewer and you can see reproductions of old models and some new designs for sale. Some people like the flavor profile of percolator coffee and also the volume. They typically make 20 to 50 percent more coffee than a common 10-cup drip brewer.

(Interestingly, Swiss Water Process decaffeination relies on a similar principle—the green beans are steeped in water that has already had beans steeped in it. Caffeine is much

Percolator

French press

more permeable than the larger flavor molecules, so the caffeine leeches out, but most of the flavor is trapped inside the green beans.)

FRENCH PRESS AND AEROPRESS®

The French press and AeroPress are full immersion brewers; all the grounds receive a relatively even brewing time. Quick and easy to use, they make coffee faster than most drip machines. The more thorough immersion gives coffee a different taste profile. Both presses add an element of pressure as the plungers are pushed down. This increases penetration of the water through the grinds and brings out more substance than a drip method. The AeroPress adds more pressure than the French press, so it is midway between a gravity drip method and other pressurized methods.

ESPRESSO

Espresso uses steam or high-heat water to push through grounds under pressure and produces a very different taste profile from a gravity drip method. Many more solids are dissolved into the water. This isn't always to the coffee's benefit, however. Some coffees seem to excel as espresso, but some produce a very poor balance or taste result. Espresso flavor is enhanced further if the coffees are roasted more slowly (so they are drier) or darker, because a drier, more brittle coffee allows for greater penetration of steam or hot water. Most lattes and specialty drinks use an espresso base, because the milk and sugar will dilute the coffee's intensity if it is not concentrated to begin with.

Most coffee shops in Europe, the Caribbean, and Central and South America use espresso machines exclusively because they prefer the taste profile. If you ask for an Americano or simple cup of coffee, they will generally produce two

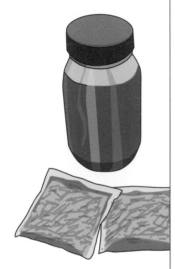

Cold brew

shots of espresso, then add hot water to dilute it to regular drip-coffee strength. The fuller extraction process creates a richer and better-tasting cup of coffee.

COLD BREW

This is the extreme, low-pressure method of steeping coffee in room temperature water for hours. It is a full immersion process and essentially an infusion. It is basically the opposite of espresso pressure brewing, dissolving only a truncated part of the full coffee taste profile and acidity from the grounds. Advocates like the lower acidity and the fact that low-pressure brewing tends to bring out the simpler essence of the grounds (I refer to this as "coffee candy"). This can be wonderfully tasty, or it might be somewhat thin and incomplete. It depends on the coffee itself. Experimentation is needed to tell you which of your coffees are good candidates for cold brewing.

Brewing Method Tips

Different coffees do best in different processes. I have not found a way to predict how a coffee will behave differently in different brewing methods. To match your coffee with the optimal brewing methods, you need to try different roast levels and grinds, and remember that what you are evaluating is how well your coffee performs with low-extraction methods versus high-extraction methods. Again, you should log your experiments and not be afraid to try new things.

ABOVE: A woman inhales the aroma of freshly roasted coffee beans.

How to Become a Coffee Artisan

The main purpose of learning about coffee is to inform your roasting process so that you are not just applying heat to beans. This final section provides some tips that will set you apart from the average roaster and help make you a master blender.

MULTIPLE SPECIES AND VARIETY BLENDING

The world's most successful and enduring coffees are blends. You will no doubt roast single-origin beans to explore specific profiles and try to find your best roast levels for each, but you should always ask yourself, "How can I make this better?" Your main tool in this quest is diversity. Not only can you mix different species and varieties together but perform multi-temperature roast blends as well.

Take the time to look up the genetics of the coffees you are buying. (The Coffee Genetics Tree in the Resources section of this book on page 151 is a good place to start.) Never assume a Kent or a Villalobos variety must be similar to a Typica because they are all Arabicas and might even come from the same growing region. The genetics and taste profiles of varieties such as Kent and Villalobos from the Bourbon branch are quite different from varieties on the Typica branch. Try balancing the acidity of a Kent with a lower-acid Caturra or Yellow Bourbon, for instance. Then reach beyond variety to add a whole different species, like Robusta or Excelsa. You are then venturing into territory that is almost unknown in the United States (but commonplace elsewhere around the globe), so your creations will be unique. A small percentage of an unusual coffee species or variety can go a long way. Try just 10 to 15 percent of something unusual, like Excelsa, Timor, or Catimor, to see how it can transform the whole taste profile of a coffee to something more complete and complex.

MULTI-TEMPERATURE ROAST BLENDING

I find that roasters in the United States typically disparage multi-temperature roast blends, believing that combining a light or medium roast with a dark roast in the same blend will create a coffee that has no dominating and defining roast profile. This is often true and can be sage advice, but blending multiple roast temperatures is also a matter of critical balance: 50/50 light and dark might create a poor cup, but 80/20 might give you a clear, defining, fruity profile with lovely caramel, butter, and chocolate notes that please the back of the palate. You may also get a different experience from the first few sips versus the aftertaste. This sort of unexpected multidimensionality can be a delightful surprise.

Multi-temperature blends are more common in Europe, so much so that this practice is often referred to as "European Roast." When you artfully experiment with the delicate balance of roast temperatures in a blend, you are not actually breaking new ground in roasting, but you might be offering something that your audience can't find locally.

Go Forth and Roast!

Take the knowledge you have gained and never be afraid to experiment and learn on your own. Keep it fun! Even the most pressured master blender working for a high-volume commercial roasting company needs to keep a spirit of adventure and willingness to try new things. When the fun is gone, so is the innovation and the happy accidents that sometimes create our greatest results!

Burlap bags full
of unroasted green
coffee beans

Resources

The Known 125 Species of Coffee:
theplantlist.org/1.1/browse/A
/Rubiaceae/Coffea

Arabica Progenitors:
scanews.coffee/25-magazine
/issue-9/english/a-search-from-within
-investigating-the-genetic-composition
-of-panamanian-geisha-25-magazine
-issue-9

Coffee Bean Standard Grades:
coffeeresearch.org/coffee/grade
.htm

Coffee Sensory Workshop:
caffeinated.training/jun29-2019
-sensory.html#1

Penagos Mill Video:
lenscoffee.com/videos-1

SCA Cupping Protocols (PDF):
scaa.org/PDF/PR%20-%20
CUPPING%20PROTOCOLS%20
V.21NOV2009A.pdf

University of Florida Taste Studies:
cst.ufl.edu/research2.html

**Where to Buy an SCA Updated
Flavor Wheel:**
store.sca.coffee/products/the
-coffee-tasters-flavor-wheel-poster?
variant

**Where to Buy an Official SCA
Cupping Form:**
store.sca.coffee/products/scaa
-official-cupping-form?variant
=14732977990

Index

Page locators in **bold** indicate a
     photo or illustration.
Page locators in *italic* indicate a chart.

Acknowledgments

I would like to thank my daughter Melanie Weisberg, who has contributed her writing and editing to all our online endeavors and assisted in the editing of this book.

I would also like to thank Pete Harkins, my roasting buddy and coconspirator, whose quest for the great undiscovered Best Coffee (and Beer) has helped me keep my sights set not on the familiar and the known but on that spot beyond the horizon where the Next Great Thing is waiting to be found.

I would like to thank the many coffee producers who provided me with images from their farms to help illustrate the beauty and promise of ethically produced, environmentally sustainable coffee growing.

About the Author

Len Brault has been writing and creating art since the days his parents had to spank him for his crayon drawings on the walls. He has written more than 200 works of expository prose and has been an art director, creative director, and copywriter at well-known advertising agencies. Prior to creating an online store for coffee, he founded and ran a design and communications firm for 17 years. He still likes to dust off his old high school Concordia Award for Journalism and the trophy the Boston Globe awarded him as editor of the best high school newspaper.

Since 2005, he has run an online coffee website, LensCoffee.com, and held many seminars on coffee brewing and roasting. He was written up in the *Vietnam Economic Times* as "the man who would bring Vietnamese coffee culture to the USA." Currently, his company supports projects to help prevent the extinction of Liberica in the Philippines and initiatives to expand the practice of Direct Trade in the coffee industry. His personal mission is to help preserve the diversity of the coffee genome and help farmers adapt to climate change through the use of alternate coffee species that can better withstand warmer conditions and the blights that can advance to higher altitudes when the climate warms. He envisions coffee as a commodity with a tremendous capacity to create improvement in millions of lives worldwide.